KELLY
This is my story
CRABB

This book is dedicated to any girl that has cried herself to sleep. You're not alone.

Table of Contents

Acknowledgements	1
Preface	2
Introduction	5
November: The Beginning of the End	15
Will We Make It Through December?	26
January: The Month of Truth	33
February: No Flowers for ME	49
March Madness	57
No April Fool	66
Hello May	77
June TRIGGERS	88
July Goodbye	95
Honest August	103
A September to Remember	109
October Surprise	116
A Different November	124
It's December Again	133
Oh January, Here You Are Again	142
The Hallway	147

Acknowledgements

My heartfelt thanks and appreciation goes to:

My Lord and Savior: I thank you Lord for faithfulness that doesn't begin to make sense. I'm thankful for the gift of grace and mercy, the promise that you are near, the strength that's made perfect in my weakness, and a song of victory before the battle is even won. Your mercy amazes me, your unfailing love has held me, and I will spend the rest of my days telling how YOU never left me.

My Girls: There are not adequate words that describe how proud I am of you three. Getting to be your mom is a constant reminder of God's goodness. Thank you for making me so proud, thank you for being my reason to smile, to try harder. Because of you I kept on going when I wanted to give up. You have always made me better, and I'm honored to call you my daughters.

My Family, ALL of you: I love each of you so much. You are the absolute best a girl could ever ask for.

Mom and Steve: You have helped me navigate the roughest days I have ever faced. Every step of the way, both of you have gone above and beyond, and have refused to let me give up. Through my tears, my anger, my good and bad, you stayed right there, always supporting us, and always doing something to help us. Nothing has gone unnoticed, not one thing, and the girls and I are forever thankful for your unconditional love and support. We love you both beyond words.

Credits:

Hair and Make-up: Hope Bowling
Photography: Hope Bowling
Graphic Design: Lucretia Kittinger
Editing Service: Kevin Anderson and Associates
Content Coordinator: Cameron Andress

Preface

I have always wanted to write a book. But like most people, there was never a day that I woke up and thought, "Today is the day, I'm writing that book!!"

I was completely oblivious to the amount of work, personal grief, and discipline this book-writing commitment would demand. It's like drinking kale juice EVERY day for breakfast, or making the bed as soon as the feet hit the floor... it's a great idea in theory, and feels like a tremendously empowering exercise. Doesn't it? I always thought that it would be an opportunity to speak without the noise of the world, an opportunity to express my opinions, or better yet, an opportunity to love the people back, who have loved me.

However, I have never felt that my first calling was writing. And I was so naïve. I thought I was saving my literary FIRST for a devotional book, a warm and fuzzy book with a cute pink cover, maybe even hot pink. I am a girly kind of girl; I will own that before we get started with this journey. Give me a cute lipstick that matches my high heels, and my day is made. I could envision this cute pocket devotional that included my favorite scriptures, and beautiful stories of grace, with mostly story-book endings.

I would have never believed that my first attempt at conveying a piece of my life would feel like a WRESTLING match with the devil, as I pulled these notes together. In place of the gathering of sweet stories and scriptures, I'm sharing my personal story of my recent walk through the corridors of HELL.

This is real. It's a bit raw. And the truth is, I made a decision to keep the content intact. It's not overly edited, nor did I sit with a ghostwriter. This is the 2021–2022 version of me: the season of tears, the season that I wanted to sleep through, but couldn't. I had to make it, if my girls were going to make it.

If I had quit, they would have quit. Sometimes we do it for the kids. Actually, most of the time we do it for the kids. That's what women do.

I have come to realize that strength isn't something we acquire through our DNA, or knowledge. Strength typically comes in the trenches. On the day when we THINK we can't breathe, we realize that we really don't have a choice, now do we?

So, the summary of this preface is simple. You're getting the rough around the edges book, instead of the cutesy book. However, I believe you will realize once you read it, that my journey through the hellish year of 2021 will be my TESTIMONY for the rest of my days. If I made it through that mess, then YOU can certainly make it through yours. That's the good news!!

God is faithful when people aren't.

I realize that this story will resonate with people who are in pain. If I didn't know that, I wouldn't bother to write it.

Introduction

Back in 2020, what now seems like a different era and a different time, I was encouraged by my dear friend Blaine Johnson to consider recording a solo album. The thought, while sweet and flattering, felt like a stretch for me. I had never deemed myself a singers' singer, or a soloist. But Blaine, being the cheerleader that he is, said, "I will help. I am in for anything you need me to do." It was as if he was prophesying our future, his and mine.

Little did I know that his stance on "I am in for anything you need me to do" would be the musical glue that would salvage our musical future several months later.

So yes, the timing was suspect, and it felt a bit like Blaine was being used of the Lord to nudge me. So I considered. Even though I had backed the greatest voices of our day, my ex-husband Mike had the reputation of being one of the most recognizable voices on Christian radio. He was a lead guy, the voice that put the rich trio sound on lots of playlists, and lots of radio programmers had his songs in heavy rotation. And then there was this: My brother Jason had this crazy vocal range and had a blazing solo career to match, my other brother Adam was the lead singer for the Gaither Vocal Band, my brother Aaron was a pastor, a double threat, because he TOO could sing the phone book and immediately bring an audience into the presence of God. He was a vocal force to be reckoned with. These guys were singers' singers. And then was the baby sister Terah. Her voice demanded attention. She sang and the room stopped and listened. So it was a crowded field, this crew I had been raised alongside, and then the man I chose to marry was equally matched vocally. After the family blended I became the middle child in the big family. My older sister Krystal, who was my biological sister, was not a singer. She was the organizer, the math whiz, but was uninterested in music while growing up. She was happy to be at home and hated bus life. I suppose the middle child position suited me, and I learned to be comfortable in that role. I felt like the solid harmony singer, but never the girl with a ton of solos, or the girl that was going to slay with my vocal. Yes, there were days that I knew that I had more in there, but I was a bit satisfied with the safety of never flying solo for too long!! The truth is, I love to be a cheerleader. I am always happy to be there, listening to the great talent that I stand beside.

After all, there WAS a pandemic, and we were ALL rethinking ways to push music and ministry forward. Blaine was so unbelievably encouraging. Why? Did he see something in me that I didn't see? I wondered. I eventually agreed to step out; my least comfortable place is OUT. And yes...there's a preach down in me, but until the anointing hits me I am thrilled to just sing. Being on the road since I was 17 years old, with the family making the decision to go big or go home, we hit it hard. Mom worked 24/7 on most days, she was the momager and the best, my kids call her a momager to this day! It's their term of endearment! Ha!! And my stepdad wrote our songs, and they were breakout songs, different kinds of songs...in a world of cookie-cutter music. So we had the dream team, in that season. Looking back as a 44-year-old, I'm impressed. It was the perfect musical storm. We weren't forced to be followers like most new musical artists were; they allowed us to create our own way. Mom took the bullets and made us the good guys, always. We produced the music, they promoted the songs, and wa-la, we had a string of a dozen #1 songs in five years. So the platform that we felt called to had been granted by a good God, and it had been somewhat earned by ridiculous amounts of work, and it was now ours. But my COMFORT was STILL in the role of support, not the lead.

But the Lord knew. And it seems looking back, that Blaine had an uncanny role in peddling the idea to me. Not many people could have brought me out of my comfort zone for the conversation, much less a planning session!! So, on what seemed like a normal autumn afternoon, we began to mold and shape a solo song list. We said that it would be a FUN project, a potential companion to a little devotional book I had considered, a perfect merchandise piece for the road, after the craziness of spotty pandemic touring returned to normal touring. So I was in!!

Now, what would be my theme? Would I look for writers to write original songs for me, would I embrace the hymns of my childhood, or would I cover all of the praise that we sang daily, as we pleaded for the death to end and this pandemic to go back to the pits of hell. It was a weird season, you remember well as you read this. Online church had become the norm, people were paid to stay at home instead of going to work, and everything in our lives seemed to be inverted. It was a very sad time in history and I suppose I was like most people: I was doing a bit of soul-searching. Death was far too common, our faith was more rattled than in prior seasons, and the saints were weary.

As I reflected more than normal, I came to realize that not everything in my life had been blessed with consistency. I've moved houses more than most, my parents were divorced more than once, and most of my adult life has been spent on a bus where I wake up in a different state EVERY SINGLE DAY! My adult normal was going to sleep most nights on a tour bus, on a pillow that was only 18 inches from the tractor-trailers that sped by. Many of those years I had an infant or a toddler in that bunk with me. The success of the Crabb Family afforded me the opportunity to be on stages around the world with my siblings. We sang Christian songs to 100,000 Muslims in Morocco, we sang at Carnegie Hall, the Grand Ole Opry, just to name a few highlights. I had the musical blessings of the village, and we had worked ever so hard as young adults. But in 2006, with the birth of my youngest child, Gracie, I left the comfort of the known. Gone was the FOR SURE paycheck, the packed out churches, the—everything provided—life of an employee, to start over. I packed up my three girls, alongside Mike, and we loaded up on the struggle bus. Mike had started a road ministry the year before with his brother and extended family. Leaving the comfort of my family was tough. But in reality, the Lord spoke to me when I was nine months pregnant with Gracie, my third child. He told me that I should not go back to my normal. I knew that the season was changing and I had to leave the nest. I knew the entire family was transitioning soon, but I was the first one out. And I didn't love it.

The season of transition had been brought on by a shocking divorce between my mom and stepdad. When he left, we were all blindsided. The season was brutal for me, actually for all of us. The pain was devastating. To try and process the loss of the family leader, the one who had co-parented this big family, the modern-day Brady Bunch that we had, was more than I could fathom. When I truly realized that he was walking away from me? I was crushed. And the truth is, when he left, he didn't look back. I was no longer a part of his life. Mom was not good, and she decided to step back and retire the brand, the Crabb Family. He e-mailed me and basically said, "You're a good girl. I wish you the best." I was gutted. The man who I was always the first to defend had officially abandoned me.

Financially, emotionally, in almost every aspect

this was hard. Numerous times I questioned God, and asked things like, "Am I REALLY supposed to be dragging my kids all over the country on a bus? Is this your plan, or is it mine?"

And then the accident happened. Fast-forward to 2010. Our bus hit a semi that was sitting still as we popped over a hill. Mike, my sister Terah, my children, and several employees were on board when this awful wreck occurred. We were doing 65 mph, and of course the accident was horrific. What should have killed us didn't. What could have been a week of multiple funerals was a week of suffering and pain with many injuries, but we were alive. My injury was a broken back. A vertebra burst on impact. Except for a tiny fragment of bone, the vertebra is now gone. I was left with a sliver of bone, directed like an arrow, ready to puncture my spinal cord. I was also left with months of recovery, flat on my back in a hospital bed in my mom's bedroom. The other injuries were devastating as well. Mike had a brain bleed and a fractured skull. Six-year-old Katelanne had broken bones and facial lacerations. She was bleeding out and had to be airlifted. When they took her off the stretcher to that helicopter it was one of the most terrifying moments one could possibly experience. They said, "Her blood pressure bottomed out and she has to be airlifted." She said, "Mommy, am I going to be okay?" I said, "Yes, you sure are." The peace of God was hovering in such a way that it was a game changer in my faith.

The rest of the crew was banged and battered, but thankfully they were released from the emergency room the same day. Mike, Katelanne, and I bore the brunt of the injuries. Terah saw it all, and her scars are there. She suffers from PTSD to this day.

The tears of my recovery were comingled with lyrics, melodies, and the memories of ministry alongside my family. They were similar to the tears of my youth. I often felt like the displaced girl, sometimes the odd man out, who didn't always fit in with the crowd. The melodies soothed me. The spirit wooed me. It was how I got saved as a teenager. Music was the key. I love the word, I listen to sermons daily, and my sermon time is everything. But music draws the soul into the room. It sets the table for ministry. And it's been a steadfast friend to me.

So as I am doing this long introduction and explaining how this collection of songs and companion book came to be, here's the entire point. MUSIC and JESUS have been my constants for many years. When I was a confused 13-year-old? It was music that was my friend. When I was in a hospital bed after a bus wreck? It was Jesus music that comforted me in the middle of the night.

In the end, I wanted this selection of songs to play like the "soundtrack" of my LIFE. Songs from every decade, songs that take your soul to the sweet place of God's word, songs that make you want to dance with joy while you're doing dishes, songs that remind you of the peace found in your grandmother's little church, songs that make you feel as if you could take down every devil that has messed with you. Yep, EVERY single one!!

And I must admit, I am beyond pleased with the process. Making this album has been enjoyable. My soul has been watered with every lyric and every melody. It's exactly what I had in mind.

And now, on to the book inspiration: The book is a bit more complex. But I will keep it short. The little devotional book morphed into a journal of survival when my life blew up in January 2021. Each month a chapter in my journey. The days of clawing and scratching in an attempt to dig out of the pit of depression are forever documented here. Again, this is a stretch for me as I step into a zone of candor that few people could be comfortable with. Therefore I admit before we start that it's a bit uncomfortable. But it feels necessary. It feels like a step toward freedom. The word says that we will be freed by truth, and we will overcome by testifying. So here goes!!!

Freedom, here we come!

November:
the Beginning of the End

Have you ever just known something wasn't right? You couldn't put your finger on it, but it was there. Like an odd feeling you got when you walked in a room? Or a weird sense of interrupting something, but you didn't know what?? And in your gut you knew. I sometimes think the Holy Ghost puts an intuitive sense in us as Christians, but this was even different than that. It was like thinking you saw "a quick look" exchanged between two people — a weirdly TELLING glance. And then you shamed yourself for thinking such a thing!! How could I think that, you asked???? How??

I have been on a tour bus singing and sharing, almost every week of my life since the mid-90s. I have known much hardship, as I'm sure you have. Most of us are in the hardship season, or we have the fresh scars of the battle as we attempt to recover from a tough season. My family has known trauma, drama, and everything in between. To be perfectly honest, the day that we left to go on the road, back when we were teenagers, was probably the day that the enemy tried to mark us. I am sure he said, "Those kids will know me, they will feel my resistance all of the days of their lives." The word says that he desires to sift us as wheat. And Lord knows he's tried. As Mom says, you can't make this stuff up. It always happens to us. She also says it's because the devil doesn't mess with people who are simply playing games and being lazy!!! He chases the dreamers, the workers, the get-it done folks!

All of that to simply say, we've fought some battles that we lost…as a family, but we always won the war. As I've told you already, the Crabb Family was blended, but even after the parents divorced in 2005? We are closer than ever, and of course my mom is a constant in all our lives, but the roll call has changed. That'll mess you up. It's still difficult for me to understand. But I always say, "God is still good." He didn't do it. We must always remember. People are people. They fail us. But I think it would make me feel better if I just knew WHY the abandonment happened. How is one's life better WITH-OUT their family?

We have seen odd behavior, and we've lived with some irrational decisions that impacted the entire family. It's not my first rodeo. My heart has been broken a time or two, and I have struggled to forgive when there was never an apology. Most of us have. It's called life. It's called the bumpy road that's not distinct to the nonbeliever. It's a familiar road to the believer as well.

But what do we do? We pack a bag, load the bus, and go tell an audience that the blood is still enough, that grace is real, and that nothing but Jesus will satisfy. I have a theory that goes something like this. The pain of the 2005 divorce of our parents bonded us in ways one could never imagine. It truly equipped us for ministry in a way that has served us. It hurt to the core, so we then realized when we stood on stage and cried tears...it was the perfect opportunity to allow the scars to show. People know what they know. We sang through tears, and we seemed to walk in a new direction with a glimpse of the anointing that was available to us if we could choose to be authentic, vulnerable, and honest. That season prepared us for the next season, which would be the on-our-own season.

And yes, road life is a constant series of listening to the troubles of people. After all, we are in the people business. That's what ministry is. We roll into town and we hear the stories of a brokenhearted momma, we see the tears of an elderly man at an altar and learn that he buried his wife the week before. We feel the pain in the voice of the pastor who doesn't understand his own cancer diagnosis. We are those people: the listeners, the people who declare healing in the face of the disease, the folks that promise to pray for the marriage that's on the rocks. That's what we do.

And yet, somehow...I missed it when it was my home. Like so many others in ministry, we push back the instinctive flashing light that's the visible warning. As I remember the "beginning of the end," I must start with a dream that Terah had on October 18th, 2020. As I write in THIS season, I realize that the Lord gave her the warning, and the ending, all for me to refer to on the hard days. It was a few weeks after the dream before she told me or shared the text, but it was confirmation that God saw the ending. I have looked at this text many times, realizing that the Lord knew way before I did, and that He had me.

Here's the text from the dream of Oct 18th: Kelly, I had a dream and I just looked it up in my dream journal. And I feel the Lord was reminding me of it.....so here goes. I dreamed that your house was flooded and the investigator said it was damned and you needed to move because there was too much mold. I went inside and the mold was everywhere....all over the walls, my heart was so heavy with sadness. But as sad as I was I looked over and could see the sun shining through the window, and I was reminded at that moment that everything was going be ok.

Later, when Terah told me about this dream in person, on a much later day, she elaborated. She said the roof was falling in from the weight of the mold and decay. She said that the outside appeared normal, but the house was destroyed on the inside, and the devastation didn't show until the door was opened. Wow!! Prophetic!!

Fast-forward to Thanksgiving Eve, 2020. Most people were still staying in small group settings, due to the pandemic. Our extended family didn't do the big gathering that year. I hadn't had Covid, and the fear that the media had created spoke to my cautionary self. Mom was in Florida and the family hadn't had a get-together in months. We had never been at home this much, working just a handful of dates scattered throughout a lonely fall calendar that was once filled with concerts and church services every week. We typically had family gatherings, often. But Mom being gone seemed to upend the big gatherings in 2020. She was cautious because of underlying health conditions.

Like everyone, our normal had drastically changed. So much time at home had given me a minute to reflect and take inventory of my life. While many people were painting their fences, or planting vegetable gardens, my attention was turned toward a sinking feeling in the pit of my stomach. It was something I dared not speak of, for it was too terrible to form into words. But I couldn't make the suspicion go away. The more I investigated, the worse it became. It wasn't looking good for this wife, who loved her husband with EVERYTHING she possessed. The marriage of nearly 23 years was older than the 20-year life I had lived before him. He had to be innocent; if not, he had cheapened everything I had said from a zillion pulpits. Basically, if he's guilty, our entire life becomes a lie. If he's playing the game to cover, I'm going to implode. I can't do it. The humiliation will send me home, I thought.

I remember well the drama from our trip to Israel in October 2018, the confrontation, the denial, and the subsequent guilt I felt. OH THE GUILT. But who could help but notice: the glance, an exchange of smiles, the inseparable bond that had been created before my eyes, the eagerness to defend the relationship, all the while telling everyone who confronted him that they were the crazy ones. The insane amount of time they spent together was commonly noticed by family and friends. However, it's a tough conversation to broach. Most of us try and reason through much of what we notice, rather than meddle. This was Mike. Everyone loved him. This couldn't be. He was a constant and so incredibly loved. He was the life of the party, a good cook, and catered to those around him when there was a crowd.

So, the Israel confrontation, the guilt nearly destroyed me. I made him cry, and I was in the Holy Land, how could I? I felt that I could never forgive myself, and I was sure he wouldn't forgive me either. The fear of confrontation without proof had totally messed me up. I learned quickly to NEVER accuse again unless I had the info in black and white, under his nose. Lesson learned. But my intuition wouldn't shut up. The little voice in my head was still talking.

So, on the evening of the 25th of November, my little family of five was preparing for the next day at home. The smell of the turkey coming from the oven was heavenly!! Christmas music was playing in the background; the girls were alive and well and making their presence known. Hope was 20,

Katelanne was 17, and Gracie was 14. I knew that I needed to soak up the days, they were growing up so fast. There's always lots of singing and you could hear them all over the house. Early in the evening, about dinnertime, I received a phone call. It was from someone we knew well, someone who was very intertwined in our lives. I had become extremely leery of this person, even though I was given no choice when it came to time spent. This person was frequently at my home, for weeks at a time, on and off. We worked together. However, that little voice in my head continued to warn me.

This phone conversation quickly turned into a personal attack on me. Now, let me just say before we get into this any farther. I don't enjoy conflict. I'm the peacemaker 98% of the time. I am the avoider of conflict. Ask my family. My natural demeanor is passive, sometimes to a fault. So this attack on me seemed to confuse my entire family. My girls were angry, so angry!!! A speakerphone conversation means the ENTIRE house heard it. And that's what kids do. They get angry because they want to protect their momma. They had the same uneasy feeling about this person and had voiced it in private prior to this night.

I was so confused. Earlier in the day I had reached out to that person to show concern during a troubling situation and to say that I would send along a gift card. The response I received was confusing to say the least.

When the call was returned about the gift card I expected nothing but pleasantries. I had tried to show concern for a situation, but my concern was rejected, and I was told that it was in fact not appreciated. What?? In all of my 40-plus years, this was a first!!

Have you ever realized that someone just wanted to blow something up, so they target ANY situation possible to detonate the bomb? I am not sure I realized it then, but in hindsight, clearly this was that, a purposeful bomb detonation. The caller had pitted me into a corner, in front of my girls and Mike. Mike's awkwardness, nervousness, was very obvious. The caller was heated, but the only time Mike got angry was when the caller suggested that I ask Mike to tell me where his allegiance was. I think Mike knew that the bomb was fixing to drop. This person yelled at me, but Mike was silent, no defense for me. It was so disappointing for us. As I look back on this night, I realize that there was trauma for all four of us; the girls were very impacted by that call. This was the night that we knew that our lives were fixing to change. This thing was going south. The truth was coming.

I slipped into another room about midnight so that I could call my mom in Florida. I told her that I felt as if a bomb had been dropped on me. I was numb. Suddenly, in that moment, I knew my world was falling apart. The tenor of the earlier conversation left me breathless.

Everything was off. It felt like a twisted triangle that I didn't choose, but somehow I was a part of. What a nightmare. And it had only begun. I knew somewhere in my soul, that the following day, Thanksgiving 2020, would be a marker, the first of a new era for me. My life of innocence was truly over. I was always the girl who took people at their word and gave everyone the benefit of the doubt. I was typically the last to know the dirt. And now, it appears that there had been a truckload of dirt dumped off at my house.

Or as Terah's dream implied, maybe the house was too doomed to save. Maybe the door was opened and now the devastation was exposed. There was a sad cloud that hovered. That was the childhood home of my children. I thought Mike and I would possibly grow old in that house. I dreamed of one day painting the brick white and expanding the closet. In my mind's eye I could see us, the couple who made it through the patches. I just knew that we would be rocking grandbabies on the deck, while singing those babies to sleep. It wasn't to be.

However, by the end of the Thanksgiving Day, 2020, I knew that I had to have the Lord's help, along with the help of a few others. But I also knew that what you don't know, you're not responsible for. But what you do know? You ARE responsible for.

I had to know. I went to bed alone, full of self-blame, shame, and a feeling that I couldn't face this. I suppose I cried myself to sleep, but as always, the sun came up and the new morning brought a fresh dose of mercy.

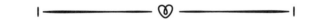

So do not fear, for I am with you; do not be dismayed, for I am your God. I will strengthen you and help you; I will uphold you with my righteous right hand.

Isaiah 41:10

Will We Make It
Through December?

After the drama of the Thanksgiving call, I settled into an abnormal "new" normal. The elephant had entered the room in a big way with the weird phone call. We recalibrated our road plans and went to tracks with no piano. After the call, the personnel change had to happen; I demanded it if I was going to be on the bus. We worked a couple of dates, and I shuffled back and forth between the obvious emotions. I would wake up in the ease of my subconscious, but face the wrath of my conscious about 30 seconds after I woke up.

And to be honest, there were moments that I pretended that things were normal, that I didn't feel what I felt or hear what I heard. Christmastime does that to people. They long for the familiar. The holidays were barreling at us, so we paused, a bit like a cease-fire in wartime. I focused on the kids for the most part.

Our transmission went out on one of those random December dates. Someone had the idea to do a Facebook live and have the family over, sell a few pieces of product, and take an online offering for the transmission. We invited Blaine over to play, and most of the family showed up. The night was sweet, and truly helped me to settle into the denial of "the phone call." After all, I would never be the one who had a marriage problem. I was planning to be married to Mike forever!! Surely this THING I was feeling would prove to be nothing. Surely it could be explained away. Somewhere in the midst of the weirdness of my unhappy days, a generous invite came that made me incredibly happy.

We have friends who knew that our dream as a family was to have a guaranteed (well, almost guaranteed) WHITE Christmas! I am not fond of taking from people, as in borrowing a beach house, a car, or even something as small as a pair of shoes. We weren't raised to take unless we worked for it. Now, if I sing for you, I will take your money. I know that I must if I'm to stay on the road. The

– 27 –

gospel is free, but fuel isn't. Of course you already know that. It takes SO MUCH money to move ministry. Mom taught me that it's spiritual to pay my people well, and it shouldn't be a struggle to buy food if you have chosen to work for a ministry team instead of a country band!! There's an entire message there, but we will save it. The point is this. I was awkward about taking this generous gift of Christmas in Colorado, but the details seemed to work. We loved the family who was taking us, and it seemed to excite my girls!!! So we WENT!!! Colorado it was. The excitement of the snow and the preparation for the travel distracted me. That was a gift!! The awkwardness was still there between Mike and me when I would ask him if he had heard from the person. He had promised to stay away, to break the relationship off. He always said there was no communication, so I took him at his word. That's my personality. I was probably in denial. But in my heart, even though the snow was magical and the girls were beautifully distracted by the travel, I feared the end was coming, soon. And how I dreaded it. I hoped for a miracle, a reasonable explanation, but faced the dread every few minutes of the likely outcome. But I compartmentalized the scenes of my beautiful girls and the mountains, feeling we would never pass this way again as a family of five.

The snow was all that I had heard it would be; the

town of Breckenridge was a scene from a storybook, or a Hallmark movie, if you will. And I shall never forget the kindness shown to us that week. The Lord knew that it would be a last, the forever memory for my girls of the last Christmas before the family would be forever fractured. This is incredibly hard to write, but I feel I must.

And somewhere in the hustle and bustle of this trip, my sweet Hope turned 21. She stayed in Tennessee with her friends and flew to Colorado to meet us on the night of her birthday. It was such an important season, overall, and yet life was so weird. And it would be weirder, very soon!!

The plan was to fly home on the 25th and have Christmas with my family, my siblings, Mom and Steve (Mom remarried a great guy about 15 years ago), and of course all of the kids. I knew there would be a big meal and lots of happy noise!! Collectively, the siblings in this big family, we have 17 children. My niece has two children, so that's up to 19. Add in all of the adults, and you've got a party!! I was looking forward to being with this bunch on Christmas Day. After all, it was Christmas. Nothing makes me happier than seeing the cousins make cousin memories on Christmas!!

While we were readying to leave the beautiful snow

of Colorado, the news of a bombing in downtown Nashville was breaking. The details were chilling, to say the least. A motorhome was parked outside on the curb in front of the AT&T switching center on Second Avenue North, in Downtown Nashville. The motorhome was carrying an explosive device. The bomber, before the detonation, played a warning audio from a speaker that was attached to the truck. A weird warning to vacate the area played for those who may have been in the area in the wee hours of the morning on December 25th, 2020. He detonated the bomb about 6:30 a.m., while children were sleeping, dads were assembling race tracks and doll houses, and moms were checking on the turkey, this man decided it would be worth his life to damage 65 buildings and injure a few locals. This was a street that we had frequented often, over the years. The Old Spaghetti Factory was there. We had celebrated #1 songs, birthdays, and other memorable events in that old building. It is incredibly sad. And I find it impossible to reconcile an act like this. Why? The story seems bigger than life on this side of history. Somehow it feels like a weird symbol of that season, for me at least. My bomb was lying in wait.

When we landed in Nashville and began to hear the stories from the locals, it was truly more than I could comprehend. Again, why? The cloud was hanging heavy over the city. Our phones didn't work. We couldn't communicate. Wow, this was so weird. We arrived late for Christmas, but praise God we arrived. It was craziness as usual; a typical Christmas, with lots of food, gifts, and that BIG family-selfie that we always take. No one knew it would be the last one with Mike.

We were exhausted from the travel and everyone was a bit unnerved from the bombing as well, so we packed up the vehicle and headed to our home. The home Terah had the unsettling dream about, the home that had been my safe space, the home that had heard melodies and lyrics to so many of our favorites as my girls sang their hearts out. I've always heard people say: If walls could talk we'd hear some crazy stuff. Well, those walls saw some sweet little girls grow up, and on this night, they saw a troubled momma drag in the front door. The unsettled feeling that would be far too common in the days ahead was resting on that house. The HIGH of the beautiful trip was waning, Christmas was over, and I knew that someway, somehow, we had to deal with the obvious!

What was really going on? Surely I was crazy. Surely I was. After all, 22 years of marriage, three precious girls, and two decades of ministry would be worth everything, wouldn't it? Surely he loved me like I loved him. Didn't he?

The day ended. I was more unsettled than I had ever been in my life. The high of the trip and Christmas was wearing off. If I hadn't had the assurance that Jesus was beside me, in front of me, behind me... surrounding me, I would have imploded on Christmas night 2020. But I didn't. As always, He kept me.

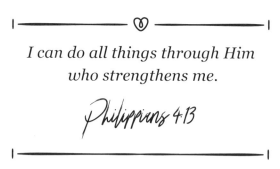

I can do all things through Him who strengthens me.

Philippians 4:13

January:
The Month of Truth

The first night out on the road, I was so uneasy. This was to be our first full weekend back on the road since before the pandemic. This was a scheduled tour with a sponsor. We had suffered financially and I was so thankful for the work. We had transitioned to soundtracks, and we were adjusting to that. However, I was seeing more evidence and the stress was wrecking my body! There are no words to describe the struggle of that weekend. I had made the decision to fulfill the dates, knowing it was going to be tough!! You could cut the tension with a knife. My confidant, my husband, my best friend...I no longer trusted. I saw the phone, constantly in his hand. The texts were flying, but they were always erased. I realized I couldn't trust him on that trip to Texas. The man who held my heart had turned his heart toward someone else. He wasn't mine. I remember where I was when I admitted this to myself. Yes, it was Texas.

Childfund was the tour sponsor, so I was the one responsible for presenting the Childfund presentation. The presentation entails me asking the audience to consider sponsoring a child who is in need. It is an amazing thing to do, and we sponsor multiple children!! Of all things, this was my first attempt at the presentation. The Childfund folks sent a representative to hear me present. At that moment I was inclined to think we should have stayed at home. I shouldn't have gone. The night before we left I told Mike to settle the girls. They have suspicions. It didn't go well. We were completely unnerved.

However, we are a bit weird. It's so engrained in us to push through, to work for the greater good and honor commitments. That "the show must go on" thing is real in my family. If you're sick, you go, if you're sad, you go. We plan weddings and funerals around the road. So, in a cloud of confusion the decision had been made to fulfill the road obligation, so I had to attempt to do so. We did our set, which to some looked like business as usual. But let me tell you, it was anything but. The emotions were off the chart. I looked over at my oldest daughter, Hope, while we were singing "Your Cries Have Awoken the Master," and she was crumbling. Tears were flowing from those big blue eyes and rolling down her cheeks. She was singing the song, and she was feeling the monumental weight of the moment. Hope, who is not overly emotional, and not necessarily prone to tears, was having a reality moment. This was probably the END. She knew. It was so HEAVY. She knew that we would probably never sing in that family configuration again, as a family trio that included her dad. It is all she had ever known, since she was born. Her mom and dad in a ministry setting, together. She took the position as an alto singer when she was only 13. She gave up her high school opportunities, she gave up weekends at home, and why? Because she believed that this was her destiny. And now? She thought it was over. She told me that she had never appreciated the opportunity quite like she did on that night, the night she thought it was finished. In her mind, the opportunity was gone, and her parents were probably finished. And she was devastated. It still brings me to tears to think about that moment; I will never forget the pain in her eyes. The night was surreal and will forever be one of the saddest nights of our lives. No words can adequately describe.

After the first set of the concert was over we went

backstage to a green room area, and that's when I knew the rest of the weekend had to be cancelled. The evidence was mounting. I stumbled through the presentation. It's almost a blur. We attempted a second half with me in shambles, Hope in tears, and Mike seemed unshaken. It was so bizarre.

As I got to the bus to speak with the representative who was sent to discuss my presentation, I felt tingling in my lips. I knew this feeling, I thought to myself. Since childhood, I break out in welts, my lip swells, my eyes may swell, when under certain kinds of emotional stress. It's an autoimmune disease, I'm told. It's tricky and tough to diagnose or resolve. It comes in waves, typically when I've had trauma. Within minutes, my lip was almost turned inside out. This would be the norm for the next five months of my life. The devil had every weapon in hell activated. My mind was attacked and my body was too.

At that moment, I declared that I was going home, whether by bus or even if I had to rent a car. The girls and I were headed back to Tennessee. As I watched the younger girls' body language, I realized that they were figuring out the magnitude of the heartbreak. I was not JUST sad, I was suddenly ANGRY. Love protects, but how do you protect from decisions you didn't make? How do you shield such a massive storm? You can board up the windows, you can hide in the bathtub, you can live to tell about the storm, but you will see its destruction, you will KNOW it's been there!!! Within 12 hours, the bus was back in Tennessee, the future was never more uncertain. The dates were cancelled. The reason given was illness.

I needed the absolute truth. Would I get it? I also needed a confession.

A couple of days later, I found myself on my cold tile bathroom floor, lying in my own tears, realizing the thing I had feared the most was true. It was what I considered worst-case scenario, leaving me with one option. My life in that moment felt like a lie, my marriage felt like a joke, and it was as if the enemy had me in a choke hold, mocking everything I had ever believed and tried to stand for. And let me be clear, when I say enemy, I mean Satan. I believe he is the true enemy, and in spite of everything, I know it was him who sought to destroy my family.

Here's how it went down.

January 11th, 2021, was one of those days that will be forever etched in my mind. As in FOREVER and EVER!! We all have those certain dates that mark our lives, the day that everything changed days: funerals, wedding, births, and let's not forget those shocking days that start normal and end with a truth bomb. I was determined to have truth, even if I didn't like it or feel I was strong enough to face it.

I needed to know. My sanity was at stake. I was rocking back and forth between feeling I knew exactly what was going on, and yet the next minute I'd be telling myself that I was crazy and a terrible person to allow my mind to think such things. And of course, it's impossible to throttle the mind when the eye sees.

On January 11th I found myself storming in a studio session that Mike was working on. The studio was at our church, and my brother and sister-in-law are the pastors. For days upon days I had been working like a detective to try and find hard evidence. My sister-in-law, Shellye, could work for the FBI, not even kidding. She gave me a crash course on digital investigation and was there to help me get through it!! Most of the people around me, who knew what I knew, were solid with their advice—"Kelly, if it walks like a duck, talks like a duck, it's a duck. Your marriage vows aren't intact. You're free to ask him to leave." However, I told everyone that said that, "I MUST have proof. Without proof, I will never file for divorce. Never. I ain't that girl."

I had prayed. I told God that I HAD to have help!! I had to have proof. Again, the phone call that I received right before I left my house was distinct. My mom said, "He's not going to confess, nor will he hand over the evidence. You have enough already. Don't be naïve."

However, it wasn't enough for me. I drove to the church.

On that Monday night I walked in that studio and boldly picked up his phone. We were in a room full of people, so he couldn't object. It was awkward. He followed me outside as I marched out the door, on a MISSION to find this thing called truth. He followed me. And the truth is this. I dreaded looking this truth moment in the eye. With EVERY fiber of my being, I dreaded. He mumbled, "It's locked. I can't get it to open." It was true, he was locked out of it, but I told him to go back to the people he was working with, and I would bring it back in a minute. I can't believe he left it. He had great confidence in my lack of technical skills.

He had been trying to get his phone unlocked, with the help of a friend, while at the studio. It was to no avail. Here's the God part of this story. I am the least tech-savvy person in my age bracket that you will ever meet. I have never owned a computer, that

– 39 –

was a personal computer for me, until I wanted to write this book. I just bought my first laptop. When I say I'm a little clueless, it is an understatement. But that night, I needed to be a savvy girl who could unlock a phone. It's amazing what a scorned woman is capable of!! I knew that I would never walk away from him, without a biblical reason. I didn't want to break our family up. I had scars from divorced parents. Divorce is hell for everyone; no one wins. I knew if what I thought was true, WAS true, I wouldn't have a choice. I desperately looked up at the winter sky, standing outside of my home church, and said, "God, You know I can't do this without proof, and I am pretty sure I know what's happening, but I have to have proof. And I have to have YOUR help!!"

I Googled "how do I unlock a disabled iPhone?" I did exactly what the first article I had clicked on said to do. With one try, the phone was opened. My heart was pounding!! I felt the fear rise up in my throat. And moments later I stood there with my answer. It took my breath away. I was holding the proof in my cold, shaking hands. An hour later, I heard the confession. There are no words to describe the pain. The torture of thinking I was crazy was over. But my shattered heart was bleeding. The panic overtook me.

The man I had loved since I was a teenager, my husband since I was a mere 20-year-old, had lied to me. He clearly didn't love me like I loved him. I was crushed. I had known uncertainly, but this was different, this was a knife in the chest moment!!

My family is a tight-knit bunch. We are a village. And anytime trouble comes knocking, we assemble and we rally, like an army preparing for battle. We have flaws for days, we're a flawed family, as are most families, but we get this part right. We know how to face the giant. Before I knew it, I had called my sister-in-law, Amanda. She's a giant slayer, a demon chaser, and nothing shocks her. I was sobbing! She arrived at my house within minutes. She was armed and ready for battle.

I had many decisions to make in a very short window of time. We had dates scheduled in three days. I wanted to crawl in bed, and stay, I wanted to find a cave and hide. I was embarrassed and was experiencing the sting of rejection in ways I never knew existed. My mom gathered the troops, and between her, and all of my siblings, they somehow convinced me to keep moving. It didn't happen the first night, but within 36 hours they were TELLING me that I had no choice. They said, "Nope!!! No hiding away for you. It is not an option. You didn't do it, and you will not give up a life that you've worked for since you were 17 years-old."

Two nights later, on January 13th to be exact, a good friend came over. Blaine Johnson had reached out to me, via my mom. He sent word that he was there for me in any capacity I might need. Blaine is a family friend, having worked for my family as a musician for 15 or so years. First for my brother and sister-in law Aaron and Amanda, and then he spent a decade with Jason. He's one of the most gifted pianists in the world. We could go six months without seeing each other and pick up where we left off. He is that kind of friend. Of course on this night, I was numb. I didn't want to visit and pretend I was okay. I wanted to hide under the bed. The girls had barely spoken a word to anyone. Sadness was thick in that house. They were in some sort of a withdrawal mood; who wouldn't be?

We were scheduled to hit the road and go sing in 48 hours, and our lead singer was gone. He had packed a bag per my suggestion. My husband was gone, my children's father was gone. I had no clue how to manage the transportation issues of the road or the management of our ministry. Mike had been completely in charge of most of the road issues. I was LOST!! Also, about 90% of our songs were out!!! Most of the signature songs from the Bowling Family were distinct to Mike. We had built a sound around him. I thought, "There's no way!!! I can't do this!!"

I remember thinking that this had to be a nightmare and I was going to wake up!! I wanted to go to bed, cover my head, and pretend. However, I couldn't sit, I couldn't stand, I paced. Somewhere in the fog of that night, I began to hear the piano... the sweetest melody ever. The girls began singing. It was a bit like hearing angels. In the midst of the hell the sound of angels filled that house. Blaine began to play "King of glory, fill this place, I just wanna be with You, I just wanna be with You." And there it was, a little flicker of hope, finding its way to me, the promise of His presence, even if you're looking at hell. Even when you are doubting, and angry, the presence of God will always find you and provide hope and peace. The Spirit of the Lord is truly indescribable in times like that. I wish all of you could have witnessed it. Music has a way of piercing the deep parts of our soul, the parts that mere words don't find.

Let me just take a moment and say, if you're reading this and going through what feels like hell, find the presence of God, whatever you have to do, stop and allow room for the Spirit. It is TRULY the only way to silence the enemy. His promises are found in His presence.

On January 15th, we had a date that was scheduled in Henderson, Kentucky. We awoke to the news that the bus wasn't properly insured. I've been in a bus wreck. I don't drive vehicles that aren't properly insured. I didn't want to go to Kentucky to sing.

I thought this might be reason enough to cancel. There were too many obstacles. And I was so scared, the girls were truly in shock, and I wasn't sure we would survive the emotion of it all. But if you know my mom, then you know. Mom said, "You're going. If you ever sit down, it's much harder to get up. Get your clothes together, we're going!!!" She came and picked us up. Determination was her friend that day!! Steve went also; he drove a truck full of equipment and product, and Blaine and John drove another vehicle. So instead of a tour bus, we had a caravan of cars headed to Henderson. But we went!! I woke up that morning with hives on my eye, plus a huge welt. I was terrified, the girls were more terrified, but they were so brave beyond their years. The night around the piano was enough to give us a few more songs to help me fill the time and reconstruct the set list without Mike. We were singing at an old friend's church, folks that I had known since the early Crabb Family days. We sat in the car until service time. At 15 minutes before start time, Mom said, "I will go tell the pastor and his wife that Mike isn't here, that it's a permanent split, and that you are fragile, but you're here. " She did exactly that. Looking back, God had His hand on this night in ways I could never explain. Clearly, He knew the day it was booked what THIS day would be. He put us in the exact place that we needed, a place of unconditional love and support. I remember the night vividly, mostly the faces in the crowd. The support in their eyes, it was indescribable. The way they embraced our brokenness was one of the most beautiful experiences I have ever witnessed. I was at home, in Kentucky. Love was plentiful. I am moved as I recall. I will never forget it.

So, the first night had been done. We did it, God had us, and maybe just maybe we were going to survive this.

That night was different musically. This sound was the unknown, musically. Blaine, Hope, and myself, as a trio, with Katelanne and Gracie singing the songs they had learned just two nights before. I watched Mom and Steve on the front row, as they worshipped and cried, in total support. Mom had committed to being on the road with me as much as possible. The last half of January was the test of a lifetime. I could not have done it without her. It was all I could do to hold myself together, to try and explain the absence of my husband to those who were brave enough to ask. But somehow,

God protected us. He put the people around us that would tell us the hard truth, yet love us enough to walk through these hellish days. Mom says, looking back, that it was like a funeral...EVERY SINGLE DAY.

January is tough to remember, and impossible to forget.

I think there was a part of me that thought this entire nightmare would turn. That I would wake up and it was all a bad dream. I knew it was a long shot, but I kept waiting for that moment of complete surrender of pride. It didn't happen. Betrayal settled in. I was so overwhelmed by the betrayal, I cried every single night, and most days too. I would lie in my bunk, cry until there was nothing left, listen to sermons and music, and continuously ask God what I could do to make this better. Some nights, I struggled to slap on lipstick and put on shoes for services. Looking back, I realized that my pain, once again, was resonating with so many women, and of course some men too. And it was painfully clear that the people were hurt and confused by Mike's absence. Many nights I saw grown men cry when the girls sang Mike's signature song, "Your Cries Have Awoken the Master." I did my best to explain without incriminating. His children were beside me. And it was so awkward for them. People were shocked, in those early weeks. They expected to see him there. There was nothing easy about it. I stood on stage after stage and attempted to tell people that my life was in shambles, but God was STILL good, and that I had chosen to trust Him even when it's ugly and messy! I said nightly, "The devil didn't hire me, and he can't fire me. I'm going on!! With or without, I am going on."

I knew that forward was inevitably the only way to go.

And meanwhile, back in Tennessee, my house felt like death. He was gone, but the house was full of everything that reminded us—his clothes, his studio gear, dozens of pairs of shoes, books, and on and on. Very soon the day came that I just couldn't do it. Thank God for my sister Krystal. She's a bit of a drill sergeant at times, but aren't we thankful for get-it-done people!! I was walking in circles, the days were foggy, and if not for those in supportive roles, I wouldn't be writing this story today. She became the big sister who was on a mission. Of course she was hurt, all of the family was suffering. This was painful for EVERYONE. My family loves Mike, but they sure didn't love what had happened. Krystal was on a mission to make sure that I would survive. She helped me go through financials; we did all of the necessary and tough things to shore up a temporary survival plan.

But the toughest thing we did that week was pack up his things. He was staying with relatives from what I understood, but hadn't come to get his things. It felt ceremonial, like a final send-off to the marriage of nearly 23 years. Living in that house was so hard for us. The memories haunted me, the loss of the tomorrow that I had planned. It was too much for me. We had it all, so I thought: three beautiful daughters, a ministry, and so many people who loved us so well.

And just like that, it was gone. By the last day of January I no longer recognized my life.

The LORD is close to the brokenhearted and saves those who are crushed in spirit.

February:
No Flowers for Me

By February we felt like we were peeling an onion. Every day brought a new, unwelcome surprise. And yet, the positive things in my life became apparent. The undying support of so many friends who sensed the dire crisis that we were in, and the fact that the girls were stepping up vocally, were the only positives. My heart was bleeding out. The girls were in disbelief. However, you wouldn't know it when they sang!!! They were killing it vocally. The younger girls became a huge part of the music overnight. Where in past seasons they had performed a couple of songs and had truly been underused. Looking back I see that they were ready to step up, but the circumstances certainly were not the way I would have hoped for.

I often stand in amazement at their natural vocal ability. It didn't come that easy for me. I worked for years to learn parts. Even now, when I am recording or under pressure, I can have a moment of nerves. But those girls have never known a nervous moment. Bring on the pressure, and they step up to the moment, vocally. All three of them are built that way.

We could not live in the house; we just couldn't. I couldn't sleep, and the mounting underlying struggles overwhelmed me. The pool liner had somehow been ripped and the pool was in terrible condition; I was never quite sure how that happened. It appeared to be vandalism, but it was difficult to know for sure. The maintenance issues grew worse daily. And the memories were like ghosts that popped out every night. The girls begged me to move. I wasn't sure what to do or quite how to do it. The real estate market was starting to be crazy in the Nashville area. There was very little for sale. And I ALREADY had a house that I was responsible to pay for, no legal rights to sell it, and a big legal mountain to climb to get there. Mike was completely unengaged with the responsibility of the house. I was drowning in financial surprises of all shapes and sizes. The realization of my financial situation was daunting, and it would be months before I could get a divorce decree and the necessary permission to sell the house.

In the meantime, Mom was recalibrating the road for us. She realized that we needed family around us if we were to make it emotionally. As only God can do, the support team was formed out of crisis. The Childfund decision makers were given the opportunity to rescind the relationship, after the terrible Texas fiasco in early January. However, they chose to support and pray. They told us that they wanted to ride out this storm with me. I was humbled and truly surprised. I weirdly felt ashamed, like I was suddenly tarnished. Additionally, my booking agent rallied. When people called in and expressed disappointment about the situation, she quickly told them that God wasn't through with me, just because Mike was gone. She was fast to remind people that the calling on my life was not negated, and that they needed to pray, and support me for not quitting!!

Somewhere in the first week of February, Stronger On Tour was birthed. The ladies retreats that we've hosted for the last seven years are called Stronger. The retreats were the organic result of Mom's book from 2015. Mom dreamed of taking this no-holds-barred type of worship and ministry on the road, for the women who couldn't take a trip and come to the mountains or the beach for the "location" retreats. The idea had been tossed around, but it was impossible to fund it the way we envisioned it. Two buses, a live band, the sisters, sisters-in-law, nieces, and any of the boys we could get to jump on the bus with us. That would mean we needed two drivers, sound crew, media, and on and on. That's a heavy price tag!! Her goal was to do one weekend a month for the duration of the year, and possibly for many years.

I'm not sure how God can move this fast, but He did. It was at lightning speed. The first week of February Mom and Steve decided that they would sell a property and buy a second bus, if they needed to. We met with Blaine, spoke to the girls in the family, and everyone was on board!! The guys agreed to be pop-up guests, when possible. Our precious friends and pastors immediately opened up their pulpits to the idea of this traveling one-night revival, hosted by our family. It would prove to be the game changer for me and the girls. Stronger On Tour would serve as a catalyst for me and for others to find our voice. Mom has always felt the need to support broken women, but in this season she was determined to offer more and do more. She knew that pouring out while in pain would resonate with so many others. It worked.

By February 10th, with Mom and Steve's help, we had miraculously put a house under contract. Talk about a miracle. I was still responsible for the existing house as well, until the end. But we had to move. The girls couldn't stay. This purchase was a miracle. I thank the Lord for family!! I also thank the Lord for friends who are there in the bad times. Think about it. We were coming out of a pandemic, a year of no work and a terrible balance sheet. And yet, the Lord made a way for us to have a roof over our heads. When it looked hopeless on the outside, when it seems we should have gone down emotionally, mentally, and possibly even spiritually? Here come the answers. Here come the troops!! Miracle after miracle, daily He loaded us down.

Now, don't get me wrong. I was walking in hell. My life was in shambles. But in spite of the ugly of the moment, provision was chasing me. People would stop me and say, "The Lord told me to tell you to buy your girls an outfit," and hand me a check. They would send encouragement daily. And the financial pieces for Stronger fell into place for Mom. By mid-February we were booked and ready to start rehearsing and roll the tour out in April. The girls and I had another ministry focus. As we said in that moment, there was a distraction from the train wreck that had become a gossip cesspool in many circles. Mom and Steve bought the bus, we hired the most amazing band, called in the family, and rehearsal began.

I had a new focus. Somehow, the Lord was allowing us to move on, in some areas of our life. And it was at breakneck speed!! This is how my family lives!! Everything is right now, let's do it. There have been times that I couldn't embrace this fast-paced decision-making, but in that season, it salvaged us. We were SO busy, we hadn't time to do anything except the task that was before us.

We grieved daily, mostly at night. Gracie and Katelanne were in school, and Katelanne was readying to graduate. The thought of that tormented me. I would have never believed that the family would be fractured!! The thought of celebratory days nearly put me in the pit. How did this happen? Why did it happen? What could I have done differently? I knew my kids didn't deserve this. They were desperate to leave the house they grew up in...it was just too hard to live there. Yet, they were emotional about leaving. There was no right answer. And all of this had happened so fast!! But as I said, the family kept me busy!!

I hired an attorney, filed the documents, and went home and cried. February came and went. I was still in shock. I was still grieving in the deepest way, and I was still texting family at midnight and asking them for prayer. When we were on the road, it was tough. But when we came home to the walls of that house full of memories, it was HELL. If I hadn't known that God was who He says He is? I would have lost all hope. I was numb. The longing to feel no pain was so real. I have a completely new understanding of those who medicate their misery.

I worried about Hope. I saw her pain and I knew she couldn't sleep. I worried about all of three of them. This is hard at best, but they were living out their pain in front of a live audience. It was incredibly hard.

Nevertheless, when I was at the end, when I was blinded with my own tears, He was waiting. When I was throwing lamps and tearing down curtains, back and forth between anger and rejection...after my meltdown...He was always waiting. And yes, I threw lamps!! I was so ashamed. I called my mom and told her. She said, "It's okay. Throw a lamp, it'll make you feel better. Just don't throw those designer lamps I gave you. Throw the cheap ones!!

So February was the month I filed for divorce and then threw lamps!! Somehow, I think the Lord understood the lamp thing.

And one more thing, no flowers on Valentine's Day!! I was accustomed to gifts and flowers, but not this year. I think I hugged the dog and cried.

The LORD is close to the brokenhearted and saves those who are crushed in spirit.

Psalm 34:18

March Madness

March came in with a roar, and left the same way!! What a whirlwind. We were staying busy, as I have already told you a few times. Those around me, my "crisis team" for lack of a better description, was micromanaging me daily, because I needed to be micromanaged!! I was up, then I would have a FAITHFULNESS of God moment, and yes...I could feel His goodness chasing me, as the song says. And then I'd have 10 minutes alone and fall apart. Relationships have addiction built into them. Sometimes a good addiction, like we can be addicted to a sweet smile, a laugh, a loving voice that is going to defend us. Those are the good addictions. And I had that going on, at times. I MISSED my husband.

HE was the one I had told all of the little things to when the kids made me proud, the one who would shoot me a look when one of them hit a crazy note, and the one I called when the toilet wouldn't stop running. All of that, I missed it. I have never considered myself independent. I married a 32-year-old man when I was 20. He had never been married and he seemed younger than he was, and I suppose I seemed older. So it was never odd to me. I had been married more than half of my life. So this separated and getting a divorce thing was NOT what I signed up for. I wanted that forever thing.

I was in it to make it, all the way. Kind of like with Jesus, I planned to go to the end of this life with Mike. Period. Looking back, I think that kind of commitment to stay married no matter what was potentially bad for a man whose priorities aren't right. He took advantage of my commitment. And sadly he knew where I was, he knew I was the child of divorce, he knew where my wounds were. He also knew what my level of loyalty looked like. He knew I would do everything possible to stay married in order to see my children avoid the pain of a divorced home. Over the years he had watched and observed my kind of loyalty. I know that marriages can go through some very tough stuff. I personally know people who have had affairs, and the marriage survived, and eventually thrived. I was not perfect,

I was flawed in many ways, but I was committed to my marriage vows, and I was committed to him. But I'm here to tell you that there are some things a WOMAN can't live with. No woman who respects herself would be able to sweep certain choices under the rug. In a million years I would have never dreamed that I would be the one who was staring at the undeniable evidence, knowing that there was ONLY one choice. Not now, not ever. There are some things you can't un-know.

We went to California to sing in March. Krystal went with me so that she could be there on my 43rd birthday!!! Mom didn't want me to be without support, so Krystal agreed to go on the trip with me. We headed west with the girls and the crew! California, here we come. I felt weird when the tiny stretches of happy settled over me. I would have a moment of it's-going-to-be-alright, only to head straight to a tearful state the moment an image or a song reminded me. I didn't know where I was going, how I got there, or when I would get to leave this place called UNHAPPY. I so wanted to leave. I so wanted to find a version of life that didn't include the constant feeling of betrayal. The thing I won't write extensively about is the girls. I don't ever want to put words in their mouths, nor do I want to state their opinions on any of this content. But what I will tell you is this. They were and are broken. They have soldiered through a horrific season, mostly without a lot of conversation. The lack of closure has been the worst for them. There's been nothing about this entire thing that's been anything less than hell. They possess wisdom beyond their years, they can smell a lie a mile away, and they are determined to be treated with respect. This awful season has changed them.

I listen to sermons a lot. I have to. The word keeps me concentrating on the answer instead of the problem. It lines me out when I'm fading into the dark place of fear. On the flight to California I had a hot sermon in my ears; it was one I shall never forget!! It was about the cross; we were heading into the Easter season and of course that is the topic for so many podcast sermons in March and April. The sermon went something like this. "Oh the cross did it, it was everything, it's your redemption!! But let's not forget the importance of Gethsemane!! For it WAS THERE that Jesus made up HIS mind!! He decided then and there what HE would do. Some of y'all need to have a Gethsemane moment. You need to DECIDE what you're going to do. Don't let your circumstances decide, don't let your enemies decide, YOU need to decide. You're the decision maker in YOUR life!!!" And whew!!! I got it. And I'm not going to say I didn't have another bad day or anything, but at 40,000 feet, somewhere over the great western state of Colorado or possibly Utah, a switch turned on in my spirit!! I MADE up my mind. I might have to claw, fight for a few things, I might have to do things I never thought I would have to do, but I was going to make it. I knew there would be some days that I would wipe tears while I proclaimed it, but nevertheless, when given an opportunity I knew I would be found telling this, "Sisters, we have to make up our mind!!! I know that we MUST be strong, for the strength that we find will be aptly passed to our seed, our sons and daughters. For in our hour of tribulation, our character is revealed. Who we are in trouble is actually who we are. And I plan to be the warrior, the girl who made up her mind that defeat isn't an option. I will not succumb to the attack that the enemy brought on my home. My house might be gone, but I'm still here. My marriage might be gone, but I'm still here. My girls may have to draw deep to find the joy of the songs they sing, but one day they will sing and dance under the freedom that the Holy Ghost will bring to our family."

I made up my mind on an airplane in March 2021!!! I'm here. I'm standing. Satan, you go back to hell and leave us alone!!!

California was good to us. We love the family who hosted us. They've been friends for years, and through this awful season of life they had been amazing. We were able to do a bit of sightseeing too. It's always nice for the girls and me to experience this beautiful country as we travel and tour. It's one of the perks of the traveling life of circus workers and gospel singers!! Ha!! This was my birthday week, and my physical stamina had been stalled by the extra weight, the autoimmune struggles that popped up every day, nearly. The autoimmune episodes were daily. The cycle was facial swelling, welts, and Benadryl. Benadryl zonks me; it doesn't make me run a race or climb a mountain. It exacerbates the existing resistance to hard things, physically. So I was not making a lot of progress with the fitness dreams. Since I broke my back in 2010, my weight had been dramatically worse. The injury of the broken back had slowed me down. I was hoping to be the girl who dropped weight quickly after my divorce as well. And if I'm being honest, I had carried so much extra weight from late-night binge eating for the last few years. I recognize as I reflect and look back, that the dysfunction of so many things in the marriage had settled in. There is a lot here to unpack. I won't go deep. However, maybe I will save it for the next book: the book about salvaging my health and overcoming the chaos of an unhealthy environment. I wish I could say that I'm the girl who handles stress with a kale smoothie and a workout. However, since I was an 11-year-old trying to navigate the divorce of my parents, I have had an unhealthy relationship with food. I was the girl who was chasing the ice cream truck or reaching for a Little Debbie when the stress hit me. I jokingly say, hand me a cookie and a sad song and I'll cry my way through. Ha!

But in all seriousness, I'm down 30 pounds as I type this. I have a long way to go. But I think me and late-night binge eating have broken up. We're finally divorced. That's a win. I haven't done that since we moved into the little blue house.

So, on the day before my birthday in 2021, Krystal and I were walking the rocky shoreline of the beautiful Pacific while on the California trip. It was breath-taking. Ahead of us was a small rock formation. It was probably about 70 feet to the top. At the top was sure to be a splendid view of the ocean. Krystal was like, "Let's climb it." I said, "I can't, I will fall." Long story short, I have the picture of us STANDING on top of that little mountain, with the ocean behind us. What a small thing, and yet what a liberating thing it was. It was an outward proclamation of my vow to make up my mind and do the hard things!!

That trip was truly a marker in my time journey. We left California, a bit happier than we were when we left Tennessee. We returned home to a house that was being emptied out; it was time to move into our little blue house. The house felt like a fresh start in that moment. It had only been 65 days since the confession, but the mental anguish was a full life-time's prescription dose of hurt. We packed boxes and were blessed to have great family and friends who helped us move. I couldn't afford movers. Krystal stepped up and asked the Restoring Hope staff and members to help. I have the best church family. She was not sure who could or would!! But they showed up and they moved us!! This story makes me cry. We rarely socialize with church folks, because we're gone all the time. We miss everything. But they were Jesus to me even though some of them barely know me. They represented Him so well!! Family and friends kicked in too, and we eventually settled into the little blue house. It was smaller, there was no pool, but we knew we were blessed to have a roof over our heads, and it was adorable!! I had a white kitchen and the most feminine décor. I truly loved it. I am eternally grateful for those who have held me up. I often say to the girls that some people go through the worst seasons of life WITHOUT support. We're blessed and we know it.

May the God of hope fill you with all joy and peace as you trust in him, so that you may overflow with hope by the power of the Holy Spirit.

Romans 15:13

No April Fools

With every drastic family change comes the dreaded "first" of the holidays and birthdays. Whether death, or the chosen death of divorce, it's all sort of the same. As I write this today, we are well into 2022, and we haven't laid eyes on Mike in more than 486 days. I will do the math for you. We haven't seen him since January 11th, 2021, the day of the confession. No one in my family has seen him. It's been sheer grief. My grief, and of course the grief of my girls, has come in waves. I struggle to think that this is a real fact as I type, but it is. The waves of sadness are occasionally coming led with anger and a lot of self-examination. Birthdays, holidays, and anniversaries, they are the worst!!! Grief is a monster that one cannot ignore. This monster demands attention.

We spent Easter weekend in Florida, and I was struggling with the next stage of removing the chains. Yes, I was getting a divorce, and yes, I had already moved into a different house and was waiting for the court date and the decision about the family home. But I was struggling with the self-imposed loyalty that I've already described. If Mike's number came up as a text, my heart skipped and I became nervous. The drama preparation in my brain was activated. And how weird is it that I somehow grew accepting of his absence, but still gave him access? The truth is, most of us use text messaging for everything!! It's used for make-up, break-up, arguments, most details that may need to be recalled, and everything in between. I was told daily by family and people who were concerned about my well-being, that I did not need a text relationship with him. They told me that I would never start the healing process. They were right. But there was such a hold on me. I was unable to refuse his normalizing of the continuation of the texting. He told me that he had a right to check on his children. I bought it. The texting was his last hold on me. My family would say, "You must stop making yourself available to him, anytime, anywhere. It's not okay to allow him access, no matter WHAT he tells you.

Let him know that if there's an emergency, you will reach out to him immediately."

I didn't listen. The texts typically turned into conflict, and the pattern delayed my personal mental health journey. He would apologize, and on a bad day, or a week that the road had been especially hard? I have allowed my mind to wonder if I could secretly meet him, if we could go underground and live, as I knew he couldn't possibly come back to this life we had. How I hated change, how I wanted my normal back. And the bad news is this... we don't get it back, and our normal wasn't really normal. But it's all I knew.

That crazy only lasted a millisecond, and it's tough to admit that I had such irrational thoughts. But here I am telling it. And the truth is that we have to give ourselves a lot of grace for our irrational thoughts that come knocking when we're in the midst of trauma. Our poor brains are attempting to reroute the feelings of love and loyalty, when we attempt to will our heart, mind, and soul, to stop loving: when we alert our innermost places that the intimacy and love was wasted on someone who didn't protect, who didn't return the vows with sincerity.

So this was me in April: Dreading the question "Is Mike still texting you?" Knowing I wouldn't lie about it, and knowing I was ashamed of the truth, I was walking with a bit of defense regarding my choice. I knew I might appear to be weak, even to my girls, regarding this. The consensus was in, but I couldn't quite get it right. So in April, here's my takeaway... we moved forward with Stronger On Tour, the legal nightmares of the moment, but the personal care of my mental health wasn't making a lot of progress.

I was firm in my Jesus-will-take-care-of-me message, we were living right, choosing the things of God, but that texting thing, it got me. He still held a piece of my heart. The texting was my only glimpse of what was, or what I thought was. After a late-night text back-and-forth, I felt guilty, yet I did it. This is what addiction looks like. It's a tough chain to cut. Addiction isn't always drugs or food; sometimes it's texting the one who is hurting you.

April 6th, what would have been my 23rd anniversary, was spent with the family, gathered around a piano, rehearsing for Stronger On Tour!! That was actually a gift to me, the distraction, the move of the spirit in the living room, and the love of family. I got through it. And weirdly, he didn't text me on that day.

Somewhere in this timeframe we had to do media videos for Stronger. There was a date set to film. We were filming at Mom's house. By this time I felt alone, single, but very unattached. The stress of the single parenting, feeling like an Uber driver, also feeling like the on property bad guy, as I barked out chore lists and demanded help from the girls. The facts are this. They were probably clinically depressed. They were not the girls who talked about it, but they were bleeding out, emotionally. I knew I had to get them into a Christian counselor, someone who specialized in grief-type situations. As we did the promotional videos, I got mad. I wasn't sure who I was mad at, but I was mad. We were to talk about the season we were in, in this video. I didn't want to talk about it, because I didn't want to be in it. Just a typical day in April, my EMOTIONS were all over the place. I was mad at the world because my life had imploded. I felt a bit crazy and, in truth, was probably in hormonal havoc, in addition to mental havoc. It was sort of the perfect storm, infused with a few nasty attacks from the demons who were still nipping at me. The facial swelling wouldn't stop. The irrational nighttime emotions were continual. That was my loneliest time. And it was so dark at times. I cried myself to sleep, night after night.

On April 8th we kicked off Stronger On Tour at Restoring Hope in Hendersonville, Tennessee, our hometown. The party was on!! The church was packed, the family was there, we sang our hearts out. The people were hungry for Jesus!!! That pandemic year had starved them; these ladies were ready for a move of the spirit. And so were we. In my broken place, I still felt the preach come over me...and it settled me in. I thought, "This is exactly what we need. The girls and I are going to feel protected, and at ease, if we're on the road with two busloads of family and friends." I was thankful. We left town and headed to Arkansas!!

We met Arkansas with excitement, and they met us with hospitality!! They started bringing cakes to the bus, congratulatory cakes for the tour, all kinds of sweet treats, and so much kindness. Wow, it felt good!! God was in this and I was so thankful for the provision of the LORD!! For all of this to come into alignment was nothing short of a miracle!! It was unusual to have Krystal, Terah, and Amanda out on the road with me, at the same time. Mom and Steve had a load of band members on their bus, and we had kids scattered on both. It was looking like we had a good day going!! Until!!!

Mom checks her e-mail about every 15 minutes, it seems. About 3:00 p.m., she called and said, "You need to come over to my bus, now." I rushed over to see what the emergency was. This day wrecked us, it threw us into war mode, as she read an e-mail she had just received. The e-mail had been copied to several churches who would be hosting Stronger;

some e-mail addresses were the pastor's personal addresses, some were the general mailbox. But the damage was done. They also copied a digital Christian music magazine!! The e-mail gave descriptive details of Mike's choices, in living color. The sender used a pseudo name, but spoke of the incidents in great detail, as if they were privy to the info firsthand. Of course, it was easy to know where the origin came from. Once again, that strange feeling of being pulled into this weird triangle gripped me: it made me sick to my stomach. It was NOW clear that destroying the marriage wasn't enough for this person. They also intended to sabotage my future. It was obvious to everyone that the goal was twofold. They wanted to silence me and my family, and they wanted to put Mike in a vise and control him. The e-mail was shocking, and within a day or so, there were other e-mails as well from the same person. They were worse than the original, in every way!! The gossip swirled!!

Mom immediately called her attorney, and I sat in silence, unsure what this was the precursor for. I was mortified at the explicit content of the e-mails. I sent them to Mike. After all, he was horrifically incriminated. But our take was this. It wasn't our circus, and we had to somehow plow through. To think I would be walking in the church that night, to minister the gospel of Jesus Christ, all the while knowing that the pastor had gotten this awful e-mail, it was mental anguish. I was embarrassed beyond words. My girls heard the stir on the bus, and we attempted to insulate them. However, we all know that kids are smart, and two of them are actually adults. I worried about them.

Nevertheless. We marched in that church, somehow we held our heads high. The LORD moved in a mighty way. Mom discussed the content of the letter with a digital team who researches IP addresses and digital forensics. I knew she would get to the bottom of it. I decided about an hour into this service that I was going to give it to God!! The impact of that e-mail was this: On the surface it was nasty toward me, I suppose. But the real content was injurious to Mike. The intent was truly to harm him, it appears. True or not true, it was injurious. He was clearly in a trap, that triangle was still in place.

A person who hides behind a computer just to destroy another person is truly the lowest form of coward on the planet. They operate in a spirit of deceit, control, threatening to blackmail those who don't cooperate. I questioned whether or not to include this story, because the e-mails are so horrifically packed with damning accusations against Mike. I would never share the e-mails, but I decided to speak of it in this book. It was a defining moment in this story. The narrative of the divorce story had been set. I didn't say a word. A computer in the Deep South, in the hands of a cruel person, set the tone for the stories that would live on. The world is a crazy place sometimes.

I am happy to report that we didn't lose a single conference, and the damage didn't reach my house. As I said, it's not my circus. I was embarrassed beyond words, but I felt the protection of the hand of the Lord and a great big family.

As we wound up this service, on April 9th, 2021, I was singing on stage, rather than working in the altars. At the time, I hadn't had Covid, and I was being oh so careful. I didn't need a hospital stay; I was a single parent! But on this night, a lady came to me while I was on stage singing.

What no one knew was a personal a story concerning my wedding rings. Mike had gotten me a beautiful aquamarine ring for our 20th anniversary. I cherished it. It was an heirloom piece of jewelry that I was looking forward to passing down to my girls one day. It was more expensive than he could afford, and it hadn't gone unnoticed. I loved it!! However, now that the marriage had imploded, it was a sore reminder on my left hand. Every time I saw it or felt it, it made me sad. So I had to simply take the rings off and put them away. It was so sad, but necessary. I had been ringless for a few weeks. I said nothing to anyone but God. While I was washing dishes a few days before, I told God. I want a ring. I don't want to buy it. I don't want anyone to know the prayer of my heart's desire. I want YOU to send me a ring. Any ring, I just want to know that YOU see me, and YOU hear me, I need that. And it's no big thing for You. You're God!! I prayed it and forgot it. If I'm telling the truth, I probably didn't have a lot of faith that something as specific as a ring was going to just show up on the porch.

Well, wasn't I WRONG!!

Anyway, the lady came up to me while I was singing. She simply said, "I don't know why, but the Lord told me to give you this ring!!!" I melted!!!! I remembered the kitchen sink prayer, the seemingly silly request, that still mattered to God, 'cause it mattered to me!! This girl broke!! What an amazing thought, just to know that God is really walking this messy stuff out with us. It's a bit overwhelming at times. Where we go, He goes. When we hurt, He bears our suffering!! She took the ring off and gave it to me. It fit perfectly!! Of course it did. God doesn't do things halfway, right? I held it and saw an inscription on it. It said, "Trust in the Lord with all thine heart and lean not unto thine own understanding" Lord have mercy!!!! This Kentucky/Tennessee girl had an old-fashioned crying spell!!! Again, for the 4,567th time, He had reminded me that He had me.

We would live another day to tell of the mercies of God, the goodness of God; it truly was chasing us. The evil was lurking, behind every rock we turned, but God was ALWAYS one step ahead. Telling me daily to choose my battles wisely and to never cast pearls before swine!! April had been good to us in ways that matter. And we were definitely living in the mindset that some things matter, and some things don't.

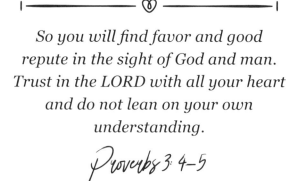

So you will find favor and good repute in the sight of God and man. Trust in the LORD with all your heart and do not lean on your own understanding.

Proverbs 3: 4-5

Hello May

Oh my, beautiful May. The month that feels like it should be subtitled "the happy month" was full of surprises in 2021. The first BIG thing was this: unexpectedly, my divorce was declared final on May 6th. It was a month to the day after my 23rd anniversary. That was the weirdest feeling. My desire to be legally unchained was strong. Strong enough that I didn't ask for alimony, even though I don't have a college degree or a way to support myself outside the ministry, with the exception of manual labor. And of course I'm not too good to work, but there was certainly a position to be taken regarding fault and the ability to earn. Mike has a respiratory therapist degree and can and has made a good living during these pandemic times. I also waived financial benefits that I could have sought. I wanted it to be over. And now it was, and all I could do was grieve.

It was also Katelanne's graduation month. I knew the transition was an emotional one for her, the end of childhood, the beginning of adulthood, all slipped into a year that I am confident felt like the twilight zone to her, just like it did to me.

After all this time of being around thousands of people, it finally happened. Kate got Covid. And yep, she got it the week before her graduation!! So in the great year of disappointment, the disappointment deepened. I could hardly stand it!! I had a pretty serious conversation with God. I whined to Him in the most frustrated way. I told Him how unfair this was to my sweet girl, how many years she had sacrificed to have a road schedule and a school schedule. I thought of ALL of the times she'd gone to school on Monday morning in serious need of a bit more sleep, and longing for a nice long bath, instead of a quick cold shower. Straight from the bus to the school, many times barreling it back to Tennessee to get her there. Such is the life of a road kid, I suppose, but this wasn't okay. For her to miss her graduation was heartbreaking. I missed a couple of road dates and stayed at home with her. I was testing negative, but I needed to stay with her, so I did. They proceeded on without us. The graduation was slated for May 15th. On the 14th, I decided to drive to Owensboro, Kentucky, for a Stronger conference. I knew I needed to drive separately, and Shellye, my sister-in-law, had mentioned that she would go with me. Hope had Covid in November 2020. But me, Gracie, and Kate had somehow avoided it. I Covid tested on the evening of the 14th; it was still negative, so we headed to Owensboro. Shellye has been a friend since we were 16 years old and sister-in-law for 23 years. She was there in the beginning, and she's still there now; she knew better than anyone how much I loved Mike. She was a part of our story, from day one. She and Jason have stood beside me like glue during this rough time. We are family, but we've always been friends too. So on this night, we left late, we were talking, and I lost track of my speed on that trip to Kentucky. I actually got my first speeding ticket on the way!! I felt a bit like a rebel. The girl who never broke the rules was actually doing 20 miles over the limit!! Oh my. Who was I? Ha!!

That week in May was about 130 days after Mike left, and I was still fighting the autoimmune junk, and the Benadryl regimen was still intact. About three days a week I would suffer the facial swelling, and of course I subsequently lost much of my day to the lethargic existence of a Benadryl life. I had been to the doctor for this condition, many times in my life. And the answer was always the same. Everyone said it was most likely the stress that was wrecking me. I was on a rat wheel it seemed. I needed to get up and move, but the facts were this. The new responsibility of the road, being a single parent, an employer, plus the added responsibility of having the musical and the ministry lead, feeling like I was flying solo? It was a LOT. I felt stuck. A bit off subject, but I was also wondering if I would ever lose the newfound insecurities. And of course the Benadryl fatigue!!! I hate to take it, but it's better than an emergency room visit; that was the ONLY thing that would bring relief. But Benadryl can't fix everything.

When the one you love has chosen another OVER you? Every ounce of hurt that you've harbored, every ounce of insecurity that's rooted in you is given fresh life. I remembered being 11 years old, when a friend of my family said to me in Wal-Mart in Beaver Dam, Kentucky, "Well, you've picked up a little weight, haven't you?" I was a fifth grader. I remember the orange elastic shorts I had on. After she said it, I remember my eyes shamefully glancing down at the orange shorts to see if they looked tighter than I remembered. And yes, I thought to myself, I do look fatter. I felt rejected and felt more embarrassment as I realized that other family members had heard it also. My parents were going through a divorce, and a little bit of my innocence was being taken with the demise of their marriage. I was the baby of this family, and as I said, Little Debbie had become my best friend. I was learning to be a "stress" eater at 11. My new friend was food.

At 43, I am still trying to unlearn these old habits. I remember feeling so disappointed in myself for being the chubby one. I remember comments like "You're so pretty, if you would just lose a few pounds." Those backhanded compliments that screamed to me, "you're almost good enough, but not quite!" Most of the time, the intent was good and meant to help and not harm, but when you are a young girl, losing your family unit, you don't understand that. So, this moment set the stage for many years of dieting, and a roller-coaster relationship with food. The shame that comes with overeating is like no other. When you walk in a room, no one knows if you had a bottle of whiskey the night before, as long as you've sobered up and cleaned up. Those of us who have a food addiction? We would never drink and drive, typically. We would not choose to harm others, not in a million years. But harming ourselves? We have no problem doing that. However, we don't have a way to hide the extra pounds; the obvious is always the obvious. The shame of the struggle is a familiar one. I long to find the key, the answer, in a healthy Christlike way. My heart cries out for a long-term solution to the problem, and in 2022, I am taking baby steps. The autoimmune situation is better. But in the hellish year of 2021, I couldn't catch a break.

The vulnerability that I felt, the abandonment that I felt, the shame I felt when my husband chose a very unexpected choice over me, took me back to feeling somewhat like that 11-year-old little girl in Wal-Mart with tight orange shorts on. Looking down in shame, heart racing, cheeks flushed with embarrassment thinking, "I am not enough." I didn't know to rebuke the enemy at 11. I didn't know that he was trying to make sure I counted myself OUT before I began middle school. I also didn't know that God was about to take a very broken, vulnerable young girl and turn her life in a direction to not only have a relationship with Him, but to walk in an appointed calling.

Over and over throughout this year, I have had to reject the thoughts that I am less than, because of my weight. If you weigh 100 pounds, or 500 pounds, God loves you and you are enough. I am a work in progress, most of us are. So, maybe this section is for all of the fluffy girls!! For everyone who dreaded summer because of swimsuits, for the girl who got picked last at the school dance, listen to me, you are enough!! Do not give up on yourself, your God never will!

I can't tell you the times I wondered if I had been skinny would I have still faced what I faced? Do I want to be healthy and in control, yes, but I refuse to let the reflection in the mirror or the size of my jeans define how much worth I have. The scale will move up and down, as it has my whole life, the wrinkles will appear more and more, but character is what defines us. God's word defines us, we are treasures, we are loved, we are overcomers, we are chosen, we are called, and YES, we are beautiful.

Back to Covid and the graduation fiasco.

I went to Owensboro and sang on the 14th. I came back home with Kate that night. I had a friend who had just gotten through Covid that volunteered to stay with her the night I went to Kentucky. The next day, May 15th, what was to be her graduation day, we sat at home. She coughed, and I cried. Her classmates graduated as planned of course, and I was devastated for her as she sat and watched the happenings on social media. What a terrible break for her.

By early on Tuesday morning, May 18th, the family was working on a plan, and the thoughts were to have a private graduation of sorts for Kate and Ashleigh, Jason and Shellye's daughter!! I was elated. We could invite friends and all of the family. The benefits of a small Christian school are amazing at times!! Katelanne's school and my family put the plan in place. My kids laughed and said that no one gets a private graduation except Hollywood stars!! Ha!! We had planned a party for all three of the cousins: Hannah, who had graduated from the public high school that week, Ashleigh had graduated from a hybrid home-school program, and Katelanne from Restoring Hope Christian Academy. So this was going to be big and wonderful. A make-up graduation it was to be!! Kate was out of quarantine, and the rest of us were still testing negative, so we were moving forward.

By Wednesday I felt like I was getting a cold, but I was still testing negative. So I kept pushing. We were readying Shellye's house for the party, and I dropped off a few things for her. Mom was there, and Shellye too. Shellye told me I needed to go home!! She knew the symptoms and could tell that I was sick. I felt sick, but I was negative and thought I needed to keep moving. Mom was dropping test kits off to me, almost daily. By Thursday I felt worse. And unlike ALL of other times, the test on Thursday confirmed, I now had Covid. Shellye's observation, as per usual, was right!!! This was my first time, 14 months into this crazy pandemic, after the thousands of interactions with people, I was positive. And it was the DAY BEFORE Katelanne's Thursday evening graduation, that we had moved from the previous Saturday!!!!

I WAS devastated. I'm sure Katelanne was too, although she didn't say it. Not only was I going to miss her graduation, I would miss her BIG party. Again, I had a pretty straight-up talk with God!! I remember saying, "So this kid who has waded through hell doesn't get to have a parent at her graduation?? Of all times, why now?? Why do I have this awful mess now?"

I was inconsolable for a hot minute or two. My family was heartbroken for me. But they did what families do. Jason thought to take Katelanne flowers; everyone pitched in and helped with her party, Aaron and Amanda, my brother and sister-in-law, pastor the church where the ceremony was held. They talked me into wearing a mask and going upstairs to watch from the green room balcony. I couldn't hug, touch, or be a part. But my eyes saw that baby girl walk her walk. She had grandparents there, aunts and uncles, cousins and friends. It was a sweet thing to behold from above. Me and God looked down upon the village who had supported and loved me and these girls. I wept. I was beyond thankful. The Lord had provided a way for me to see it all. The Lord knew that in this moment of my life, I needed the perspective from the balcony, more than the view from the front row.

I went home and went to bed, cried a little, and waited for pictures from the party. Meanwhile, across town at Jason and Shellye's, there was a big family party going on!! Special cake, party dresses, beautifully wrapped gifts, tons of family and friends, and a warm Tennessee evening seemed to be nothing short of a gift from God to these three "cousin" graduates, who had been together literally their entire lives. They started kindergarten together, and on this night, they laughed, posed for pictures, and had a sweet opportunity to celebrate their achievements!!!

And while they partied, I was tempted to throw my own "pity" party. After all, I was alone, sick and missing out. But the overwhelming lesson from the balcony, the view of the support and love, was my lesson of a lifetime. It wasn't what I wanted, but I knew that the Lord had taught me something. So that's a win.

I keep my eyes always on the Lord.
With Him at my right hand,
I will not be shaken.

Psalm 16:8

June Triggers

The saddest thing about betrayal is that it never comes from your enemies. I'm not sure who to credit this quote to, but what a cold, hard truth it is!! As I told you in the May chapter, the divorce was final before summer rolled around. I was in the thick of trying to navigate this newly acquired officially ALONE status. My days were a mixture of thankfulness, devastation, sadness, and a large quantity of confusion. The "why" was a looming question, always underscoring every good thing, and the humiliation wasn't going anywhere for a long while. It was ever present. My life is a public one by choice; although not on a large scale, it's still out there in front of people. Trying to decide how to handle such a train wreck of a situation, in front of people, all the while trying to protect my girls, has proven to be one of the challenges of my lifetime. How do you tell your story of betrayal without making the other party look bad? I decided to share, but not overshare. It's amazing how people will force you to walk through hell, and then suggest you put a muzzle on your mouth. But here is a dose of truth!!! Your story is your testimony! My story is my testimony!!! I knew it was a miracle that we were still standing!! It was ONLY the hand of God that steered me away from the pit of a deep, dark depression!! That same God had given my three sweet girls the courage to keep their heads up!! And as for me and my house, we were hanging on to every promise of God, in spite of the mountain we were climbing.

But life was life, and we were so vulnerable. A trigger could change the day, on ANY given day. Such was the case on June 11th. First of all, the 11th is a trigger. I'm sure it always will be. It was on January 11th when I got the confession. The awful sound of his voice, admitting that my worst nightmare was reality. The worst sound my ears have been subjected to at this point in my life. I have no words. So, on this day, there were actually two triggers.

We were in Boaz, Alabama, with the Stronger Tour.

I had dreaded it because it was the town where I met Mike. I was a mere 17-year-old, as green as grass, just a country girl from Kentucky. We were there as an opening act for the group Mike sang for. He told Jason that he wanted to meet me. From the moment we said hello, I was smitten!! You know the rest of the story by now. When I was 20, I married him in a storybook wedding in my hometown. He was my forever love, my favorite singer, and the father of my beautiful daughters. He was all of that. I loved him, I loved his family, and I loved what I thought we had.

So on this night in that familiar Alabama town, I kept telling myself that I was fine. However, I was far from fine. As I sat on stage, surrounded by my daughters, nieces, and sisters, I absolutely broke. It was as if the floodgates had been opened and I couldn't hold back the tears. Okay, this was the big one. And it was in public!! A river was flowing, tears were streaming down my face. I felt the panic that can only be understood by one who has had a breakdown in front of a packed-out crowd!!

I could see my girls were concerned, and I had no choice but to exit the stage and go to a little room on the side of the stage. The crowd was confused. No one knew what to do. Mom and Krystal were on the front row in the audience. They explained later

HOW confused they really were. Mom wondered: Should she go check on me and disrupt the entire evening with the drama of the exit? It was a Stronger event, and if she had gotten up and walked out, she thought it would make an awkward situation MORE awkward. It was a tough call, and the audience knew it was bad!! She sent Krystal. A little less obvious, I suppose. I was in that room praying up a storm, rebuking the enemy of my mind who flooded me with memories!! I prayed, "God, please help me, if You don't I won't get through this night!!" As the tears continued I realized I couldn't stop them!! I was HELPLESS!! So I submitted to the moment, even though it was at the most inconvenient time imaginable!!! I crumbled in that little room in Boaz, Alabama. Krystal walked in to check on me, all the while they were just a few feet away on stage, singing and sharing. I was mortified that I lost it like that, but grief was the boss on that night, and pride is no match for grief. So now there are two Boaz nights to remember. One sealed the beginning, and one sealed the grief of the end. Such is the circle of life. We start and we finish.

I somehow managed to pull myself together and go back in time for my portion of the night, where I typically speak to the audience. I don't usually get extremely nervous, but my heart was pounding, my thoughts were racing, and I had no idea what I would say!! In fact, I don't remember a word that I said, but I do remember that God met me there and was my help!! Just like His word promises He will be. I am always astonished by His timing. And may I remind you of something right now? His strength is made perfect in your weakness. Always.

After the breakdown in Boaz, Krystal planned a little "sisters" getaway for the two of us in Birmingham. She surprised me with a spa trip at a beautiful hotel!! It was kind of a first for me, and it was a great getaway!! It was astonishing how it felt for me to clear my head and escape. It consisted of the best French food I have ever had, a Kate Spade purse purchase, and lots of much needed laughter. I love how life is with sisters; you can be the real, raw, the dorky unedited version of yourself, and it's always okay. They are going to love you no matter what. My sisters are truly my best friends.

Our first morning there, I got a call from Mom wanting to discuss our bus. She didn't care that I was on a vacation, ha!! She's always ON! Let me explain the call. We spend anywhere from two to four nights a week on a bus; it is our home away from home. This bus, we had been in since 2011. There were many memories attached to THIS current bus, mostly recent and mostly bad. The girls and I were struggling. Knowing what we now knew, it was tainted in many ways. When the enemy comes right under your nose, it's a unique perspective, and an icky feeling when he is brazen with his tricks. We had been attacked in our safe space, and it was hard to ever feel the same in that space again.

So, on this beautiful, sunny day, as I was about to go to the pool and enjoy my little day of escape, Mom is asking me if I really want to sell the bus. She knew the mental health of our family would improve with a change. I went with my gut and said, "Post it on Facebook." I then put my phone in my bag and walked down to the pool. I found a good chair to relax in and said a prayer: "God, if it's Your will, let it sell quickly." The truth is, big decisions tend to intimidate me, especially in this new season of being the only one who makes them.

Within hours, Mom was calling me back; as I answered the phone, she said, "You're not going to believe this!" I asked, "What?" knowing that in this season anything was possible. She then told me that someone had already made an offer on our bus!! In fact it was precious friends from Mississippi.

I was once again amazed at God's faithfulness and His attentive ear to my needs. We proceeded with the search for a bus; in the meantime our family home was listed and sold, and just like that, the new was shaping into its own season, and hope was alive in my heart.

And yes, I believe that there will always be triggers that mess me up. But I can't live my life based on the emotion of my memories!! I must live in God's purpose for me. Devil, you have no hold on me! And Boaz, Alabama, if I ever get to go back, I will enter the city shouting, for the LORD has kept me!!

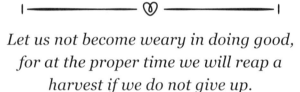

Let us not become weary in doing good, for at the proper time we will reap a harvest if we do not give up.

Galatians 6:9

July Goodbye

July 1st, 2021. What a significant day in my life. Eleven years prior, we had survived a horrible bus wreck. Anyone that knows me knows the story. I have shared the story at least a thousand times, of that fateful day!!! The day that would bring life-altering changes. The bus wreck in 2010 left me in a back brace and a wheelchair for six long months. Katelanne, my middle child, was life-flighted from the accident!! She was bleeding out from a deep laceration that had ripped her face open and left her fighting for her life!!

She also crushed her clavicle. There's been much said and written about this day, but I can't omit it from this book. For it was a marker in my life. A stone was placed to remind me. I also have an aching back to remind me, especially after I've been on my feet all day!! But the miracle of being on my feet all day doesn't go unnoticed. The doctors weren't sure I would ever be physically able to stand on stage long enough to do a full set list. And they also warned that I may never wear high-heels again. But Praise God, I can do both every single week!

We didn't sing a handful of times that year, for I was in a wheelchair, and we weren't sure if our injuries would allow us to ever travel a normal touring schedule again. My L1 vertebra burst upon impact, as my feet smashed into the end of my bunk wall. July 1st is always my "I lived to tell about hitting a semi" day!! It's a praise day. Mike had serious injuries as well. It is a miracle that everyone on the bus lived!!

I am also reminded on this day, that an accident like this one could have killed us. A bus that's going 65 mph and hits a semi that's sitting parked in the middle of the road, logically that accident should have fatalities!! But God!! On the seventh anniversary year, I marched around the bus seven times, in the thickest Texas heat you could imagine!!! Different bus of course!! We were parked on a ranch where we were set up for a big 4th of July shindig/

concert. I felt the march, so I did it. We never know what kind of miracle our obedience will unlock. It doesn't have to make sense. God things don't always make sense!!

July 1st was certainly one of those days that marked my life!! There was a definitive before and after!! We all have them, the days that come to proclaim you are never the same. I made up my mind during that long, horrifically painful recovery, that if I ever got through it, I would tell it. If I ever walked without a walker, if I ever sang a whole set standing, if I ever went a day without horrible back pain, I promised to always remember where God had brought me from. The day is always somewhat emotional, but as the years have passed, the emotion has turned into a grateful kind of day.

After experiencing that kind of trauma, one is simply appreciative for the little things. It might be a little God wink that on the 11th anniversary of this significant day, that our bus we had decided to sell in June, left the parking lot in Goodlettsville, Tennessee!!! She was on her way to the new owners. We had so many emotions as we stepped on "big blue" for the last time. My girls had been raised on that bus, they had done hundreds upon hundreds of hours of homework at the front table, they had argued like sisters do, and learned to sing parts in the back room!! I had mothered them through some very formative years on that big blue bus. I prayed over it, one last time, believing that the sweet family in Mississippi that it was going to would be safe and that they would make many great memories while traveling, and that it would serve its purpose for them as well.

Another piece of what was, was now gone. It had to happen, but it was bittersweet. The house? Was the same. It had to happen. As Terah dreamed back in 2020, the decay had set in. We felt as if the charade was acted out in that house and on the bus. We couldn't stay, but it was STILL a tough day. We drove by it one last time, and it was tough!!

I had to remind myself, that life is not going back to what it was, that's not how this thing works. That thought still wrecks me on certain days. Sometimes, starting over is the only way to God's best for you. That blue bus rolling down the interstate on that final day felt like an invitation to let the healing ramp up a notch or two, for all of us.

I tend to resist change; it's part of my personality. It makes me uncomfortable at my core. However, transition is a big part of life. Walking by faith is part of the assignment for every believer. A new bus was going to be in our lives soon, or new to us, and that was something to rejoice in. So on the celebratory day of survival, me and these girls thanked God a little louder, and we allowed ourselves to look ahead.

As that Kentucky blue Prevost headed south to Mississippi, I was turning another page.

We finished out the month with the fortitude of this new normal!! We took off the week of Overflow, our annual church conference, that's truly a big revival!! I knew I needed it, I needed the downtime, and I needed to hear from God. Clearly the change that had been dictated to me wasn't on me. I hadn't chosen it. But the rest of my life couldn't be spent playing DEFENSE. The word says to cast a vision, to write it down and make it plain!! In other words, let the world see. Pray about it, but then: Declare it and walk in it. I knew that the Lord would be my rear guard. I was trusting Him to defend my right to continue living my life. I have witnessed other ministries who faced personal devastation. Some of them allowed the devastation to destroy God's perfect plan for their lives. They stopped, found a sofa, and quit. While others were wounded, and often I've seen them bandage up, stop the bleeding, but then? They get up. They turn the very thing that came to kill them into the weapon of choice for the next season. In other words, the test became their testimony, the mess became the message, the trial became the triumph, the victim became victorious!!

Along about July, I began to ask myself; Am I truly stronger than I thought? Could I possibly be one of those stories in the making, the girl that's blindsided, on the floor with grief in January, and yet I'm seeing the glimpse of morning, the daylight that brings confidence that the sun's going to shine.

I felt the need to clearly consider my future. The ministry goals, the financial goals, the options for me and my kids were in God's hands, of course. But I needed to realign the vision. Mike was gone. And we had been playing a defensive plan all year, total survival mode. Now, God was saying to be intentional. It was a game changer.

I don't struggle with listening. I take advice with ease. I'm a rule follower. Many would call me a chicken, and I suppose I have been at times. But in this moment of my story, I had found an abandon down inside that mirrored bravery. I had also found a deep desire to glean advice from those who knew the severity of my situation. I desired wisdom to go along with strength. We must have both. Wisdom is often the key that's missing in ministry, I am aware of that. The calling, the anointing, the talent, all of the things can be intact. But without wisdom? It's often a train wreck. I was looking for a life that was rooted in God's purpose for us, and I was determined to make good choiccs so that we could have a solid future.

So much of the time we allow exhaustion to creep in; the spiritual desert of physical exhaustion is a real thing. Our bodies are worn out, and our spirit man/woman becomes weak, tired, and the world starts to be cloudy. Back in January 2021 when Mike left, I made a decision to take off the week of Overflow, so that I could be renewed. Innately, I knew I must. All those months before, I knew. I blocked the schedule and we stayed at home.

The week of church was everything!!! After the year of hell that we had, I was raw and came ready to receive. I didn't need anyone to pump and prime, I was ready to hear from God, and my goodness, I did hear from Him!! Wherever the truth is welcome, wisdom shall spring forth!! I was ready. The year had made me tougher for sure. And I had learned that there was a new fight inside me.

I know I must pick my battles, but some things are worth voicing an opinion, explaining why you have it, and then standing your ground!! On to August!!

The nations will see your vindication,
and all kings your glory;
you will be called by a new name
that the mouth of the Lord will bestow.

Isaiah 62:2

Honest August

There will be days that you have to be your own cheerleader. I think most people enjoy a good pep talk. I know I do!! And oh my goodness, they are so necessary at times. My mom is the queen of giving a good pep talk. She can convince you that you can do anything in about 10 minutes!!! And let me tell you, there have been many times throughout this process that I have hung on her every word! I would find myself clinging to every detail of what she said, hoping it would sink in and I would miraculously wake up to the things she told me I was capable of!!

I would cling to the hope that people spoke over me. To get through heartbreak, rejection, the loss of anything significant, we must have hope: Hope that is greater than things of material value. It's the Jeremiah 29:11 kind of hope. "For I know the plans I have for you, declares the LORD, plans to prosper you and not to harm you, plans to give you hope and a future." We read it over and over when we're in the mess, soaking in the message that God has a plan for our messed-up lives, that He has a future that is good, and even prosperous. That is the darkest hour kind of hope!! It's the thing that we grasp while in the thick of the pain.

By August, that kind of hope for my future had taken root. I was able to think in a forward way, without wanting to talk about my broken heart. It was truly a new season in many ways. We needed a new publicity photo. We had been using one that was cropped from an earlier shoot with Mike. I hadn't had the heart or the mindset to care about a new photo, until August. We booked a session and did it!! Sometimes it seems like the little things are big things. I dreaded a photo shoot so much.

Additionally, I had always dreamed of the girls making a Christmas album. But in the mess of 2021, finishing anything was impossible. As I said earlier, we were in survival mode. Life in 2021 had been a series of days where we put out fires, dried tears, and reacted to the things the world threw our way.

It was little more than that. Survival! But the shift had happened at Overflow.

In particular was a moment, a random thing that felt significant to me, and maybe no one else!! Bishop Kevin Wallace had taken the platform to bring a word. I believe he had opened with a scripture and was starting to exhort, when suddenly, he pointed at me, And he said, "Kelly, God knows about this. And you have a new name!! Don't worry about it."

What he couldn't have known, and what no one knew except a couple of people, was this. It was suggested early in this transition that I change my name to Crabb for the purpose of identity with our core audience. A music attorney gave that advice to me, over lunch, early in 2021. Mom was there, and we both rejected the idea. He said, "I've known you for 25 years, and I know you only by Kelly Crabb Bowling. If you ever plan to drop Bowling, do it now. Go to Crabb." We didn't agree, and we moved on. Advice is always welcome in my world. I ask for advice about most things, and I typically take it. I AM THAT GIRL. But this felt awkward. Gerald Crabb isn't my biological father. He was my stepfather for 15 years. When he and my mom divorced, Mom retained the name. It was her brand also, her years of work to establish the name. But for me? It felt disingenuous on the surface. My biological dad is alive and well, and my maiden name is May. I am the daughter of John Paul May. We have a good relationship, so there was that.

My dad had remarried and I had a much younger half-sister, Taylor. We were on the road so much in those days, and I was grown when she was born, so we didn't technically grow up together. But I love her, so I also wanted her blessing. She too had the maiden name May. Would it hurt his feelings? Would it hurt hers? Would I live in regret? And the choice very felt permanent. After all, most people don't change their name every other year.

Bishop Wallace couldn't have known that this topic had resurfaced, and every person who had experience in this area agreed. Kelly Crabb was the answer. The arguments were sound. The name is your musical heritage. You were on every single Crabb Family album, you were there from day one, and that is your family. "If you change your name as a result of divorce, you must do it now" I was told OVER and OVER!! It won't feel like a natural decision in five years. We were revamping the social media platforms and applying for the changes to add the girls onto the name heading. There's lots of red tape and it's difficult to get these changes approved. The Bowling Family felt odd for the sound of those three girls. I knew we needed to make the name change and add them since they were there singing their hearts out, nightly. It was also pointed out to me that the musical name "The Bowling Family" carried an association with Mike's many songs, and that there would be musical confusion until the straightforward name change happened. For the sake of transparency for the current musical style, it was the time to make a permanent change. If I were to decide to change my name to Crabb, I felt incredibly worried about my dad's feelings. He had never been active in my music career, but he was my dad, and I cared about him. It mattered to me.

The final argument was this. Okay, if you decide to stay Kelly Bowling, you don't get to change it later. This social media thing is a bear!! They may not allow another change. When your girls get married, you may be the only Bowling left on that stage. That hit me like a brick. The last comment was this. They said, "This is the year you must think about YOUR family, your calling, and your future!!"

That was a few days before the service with Bishop Wallace. I had my answer, and man didn't give it to me. God did. Mom was on board. She had been for some time. I called my dad next and he unselfishly told me that he understood. I love my brothers, and I love my sisters too. I felt nothing but support, maybe even some pride from them. I think they were proud of my boldness, maybe?

So in the month of August, at 43 years old, I received a new name. My musical heritage was cemented on my bio. And I retained my maiden name too. I wear my name with pride, and I was surprised by the freedom that I felt when I made the change. I am at peace with the decision to be Kelly May Crabb. After I did it, I felt liberated in some odd way. I think I felt brave for making the choice to do what made sense, felt right for my future, in the face of the fear of judgment or rejection.

People-pleasing is truly a trap at times. I've done it most of my life. However, I have learned this: people-pleasing is rooted in fear and is focused on earning love. And when you have genuine love, it casts out fear. I am learning.

There is no fear in love. But perfect love drives out fear, because fear has to do with punishment. The one who fears is not made perfect in love.

1 John 4:18

A September to Remember

The girls and I had been in a lease bus since the first day of July. As I've already said, we spend more time on a bus than we do at home. Therefore, we were anxious to get our bus. It wasn't new, but we had purchased from Hemphill Brothers Coach, and the customization process on any bus was their forte, be it brand spanking new or a refurbish that's a few years old. The truth is that we were in a crazy season of bus shortages. During the pandemic a large number of fleet buses had been sold into the private market, and people had repurposed them for motor home usage. All of that to say this, the bus hunt hadn't been an easy one. I had lots of help with the process of finding something that was in budget, yet in good condition. It took us a minute to find a good bus, and then the refurbish was slow. But hey, we had waited for it. We were pumped about it!! It's a big deal to those of us who practically live on the road. Most people have house envy!! But many traveling folks have bus envy! Ha!! When an artist gets a new bus with all of the updated amenities, we love to tour and celebrate with them. It's a big deal! We were in that awful homeless stage of the wait.

The crew had faithfully moved equipment back and forth, from one leased bus to the next, a few times during the summer. We toted our clothes, shoes, and every single thing we have to have to travel, back and forth as well. So the year we moved houses, we also moved buses. But the bus moving was a bit more involved than it sounds. So the hot, sometimes hellish summer of 2021 was nearing the end!! And our bus was finished!!! Goodness, the girls were giddy.

September was the month! The call came. It's almost finished. You can expect delivery tomorrow!! And yes, it was worth the wait. The shiny exterior glistened on that September day. My brother-in-law Jon was driving the bus around the building; he works for the coach company that customized it. When I saw it, I realized I was going to have a moment!! I couldn't believe it. I broke. Had God really done this for us? Without new music to sell, without the financial help of an investor, had we really been able to do this?? The faithfulness of God was on full display as that beautiful Prevost came toward me. Tears and more tears.

The custom shower for the girls, the built-in make-up station with a bench and a homework table that adjoined it, the backroom comfy bunks for me and Gracie, and the private section for Hope and Katelanne in the next section forward. The first section was privatized with custom dividers for the crew, better known as the guys. This is the first bus we've owned that had a true guys and girls section. I was more thankful than words can describe. I felt the lyrics of the song that says, "Your goodness is running after me."

The shock of the tangible evidence of God's provision was settling in on me. How had we survived financially? And how in the world had we bought a bus? If I could tell the entire story, you would be in shock. Even though we often speak blessings over our own lives, we learn to be our own cheerleader in the darkness of night, and we quote the promises over and over, like the result will be better if we say it more. We pray over everything we do, especially when we're in a season of yuck. BUT we are ALWAYS shocked when the evidence of HIS faithfulness rolls onto the property. On that day, the evidence was a 60,000 lb. vehicle that would be a rolling home to me and these children. And she was a beaut, Clark, if I can quote Uncle Eddie from Christmas Vacation!! Ha!

A Prevost is probably not what YOU have need of. This miracle may not resonate with you. You may be praying for a house, a car, a call from your estranged child, a good report from your doctor, a miracle in your marriage, or maybe something so intense you could never speak of it. I feel that I should stop right here and simply say. God doesn't love me more. If you haven't seen your provision yet, don't stop asking. It's rolling your way. Don't stop working toward that thing that you desire. Keep pressing, God isn't slack, He will not fail you, or me, or anyone who finds themself in need of a miracle!

The days were short and the nights still felt long. I was officially single, unattached, and uncertain of my tomorrow. The confusion of not having the ability to IMAGINE my tomorrow got to me at times. I had nothing to replace the mental images of my future that I had imagined for many years: ME and Mike, rocking chairs, grandbabies, and all the things. My life felt so complicated now. Would I ever love again? Would anyone ever tell me I was pretty again? I mean besides friends and family, you know, a man, a Godly man. Would there ever be a man who understood my life? A man who could understand the dynamics of my messy situation, a man who could understand that my girls are withdrawn and bruised? Would there ever be a candidate who was also brave enough to embrace the crazy schedule of a touring family? Let's be real here. I don't have the ability to go to a hospital and get a job as an RN. And that's okay. God called me to an evangelistic ministry. I sing and I speak. It's been my life's desire to walk in this calling, for it is here that I feel that I'm in the will of God. That's why I stay. Sometimes that's the ONLY reason I stay. Nothing about it is easy, but it's worth it.

But if we're being completely honest about this topic, I feel that the average single guy in my forty-something age group, you know, the guy who works at State Farm, or the local bank, they're looking for a girl who is a nurse, or a teacher, or anything that's attached to a regular stay-at-home schedule. The traveling aspect of my life, in my mind, would complicate any relationship with a man who had office hours and a career. No one wants a wife who is gone all the time. It would be impossible to help him parent children, if he had children, if I'm absent more than not. I know you think I'm eliminating most people by feeling this way, but what I am saying is true. My sister-in-law said it this way.

She basically said: "It's tough to marry into this family anyway. We've all been together for so much of our LIVING. The life experiences of the tight-knit family make it tougher on the newbie, the one who wasn't there. That's for starters. And then you factor in that no one could POSSIBLY understand the complexity of the schedule, the undying family loyalty, and the submission to ministry that always comes first. IT IS A LOT!!"

We are the family who had a GREAT result with a blended situation. But that was then and this is now. Now, I will say. God can do absolutely anything!! I will not rule out God's plan, but it will have to be God. The candidates are few, the way I see it!! The circle is small. And yes, I think I've been far too honest in this portion!! Who knows, I may marry a man with a nine-to-five job and three-year-old triplets!! HA!!

Truthfully, at this point in my life, I can't imagine marrying anyone. But I will certainly keep you posted! Ha-Ha!! What I do know is this. God has a plan and I'm looking forward to it.

The last thing about September: Katelanne, my sweet middle child, turned 18. Somewhere in the busy, sad, blessed, confusing year of 2021, this sweet girl became an adult. The celebration was minimal, but the love was BIG. She's the quiet one, the one who has the artistic eye of Monet and the vocal ability of Celine. I know I'm her mom, but I've never seen anyone like her. When she finds the confidence to step into her ability, look out world. So we ended the month celebrating my little Kate-Kate and thanking God for these beautiful girls. I say it often: If I have endured the heartbreak of this season, I would a million times over, just to be allowed to be their mom. They're worth everything. No price would be too much.

There are no words to describe the way my heart feels when I hear them sing, when I hear them use the gifts that God gave them, especially in this season. They don't have to, they choose to. It's my most prized role, being Mom to them.

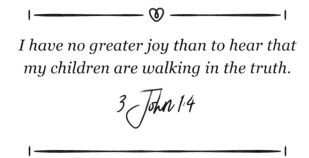

I have no greater joy than to hear that my children are walking in the truth.

3 John 1:4

October Surprise

October started off with a bang!!! A very unusual thing happened. Now let me set the stage for this day being referred to as unusual. The ministries of our family have never been easy to put in a box and label. I am sure there is a complicated answer for that, but I won't go into it real deep. But a for instance, back in the era of 2000–2006, the Crabb Family was selling out buildings, selling hundreds of thousands of records, and yet, we didn't have the ability to win a Singing News Fan Award.

Let me explain: We (The Crabb Family) had won Dove Awards, we had Grammy nods, we had lots of #1 songs in the Southern Gospel genre charts, but the award that was synonymous with Southern Gospel, the Singing News Fan Award, typically evaded us. Actually, it always evaded us. We didn't fit the mold to perfection, and we knew it. Let me be clear. We didn't care. We don't work for applause, we stick to working for a cause. I respect the awards process. It's always an honor to have the hard work be noticed. Awards also honor the craft, and that's always nice, but we don't count awards. I have no clue how many we've won, or not. I can tell you that there's not a person in my family who has ever bothered to count them or talk about them. It's simply not our thing. As a matter of fact, our song "My King" won a Dove Award in 2021, and we didn't know it was nominated, so we weren't there to accept. That's almost embarrassing to admit, but it's true.

Back to October 1st. A close friend, who has watched the progression of many careers, insisted that we go to the Singing News Fan Awards. She said she had a feeling that my daughters would win!! Most of you know that they make music separately from me and sing as a trio on the road. Hope does double duty: she sings with me and her sisters. I'm sure that that will morph into other combinations, with time. But in the present, the girls have a wonderful trio and they tour with me. In 2021, they were nominated for Favorite New Artist as the Bowling Sisters, and Hope was nominated for Favorite Young Artist, an award that was for singers under the age of 30.

Somehow the opinion about the girls winning resonated with me, so we loaded up and drove to Pigeon Forge, Tennessee, on October 1st. The girls didn't understand it, and neither did I, in one sense. But the love of people had been flowing like water, and this was the only year that these awards had allowed online voting. I knew all of that. As it turned out, the girls had the surprise of a lifetime. They WON!! They felt loved, embraced, and the timing couldn't have been better!! Hope also won the Favorite Young Artist Award. She was absolutely shocked!! And so was her momma!!! In a weird way, it felt like a full circle moment. We haven't been to the National Quartet Convention in many years. That is a convention that the artists in the Southern Gospel genre, the genre of our family's musical beginnings, consider the flagship event of the year. The award show was held during the convention. We (The Crabb Family) dreamed of singing there when we were kids. It was the highlight of our year to attend as teenagers, watching from the cheap seats, hoping to one day be invited to perform. And God did all-of-that plus so much more!! But on this day, here I sat. I hadn't been in this building or sang for this event in seven or eight years. These were the people who loved me when I was Hope's age. These were the people of the early

Crabb Family days. And on this beautiful October afternoon, they honored MY girls with honors that seemed so very random, so unexpected, yet so appreciated and humbling.

I am fully aware that outward success will never give us inner peace. People will accept you, and then change their mind and reject you. You will be wanted, and then you'll be ignored. It's life. Ministry is no different than any other occupation, as it relates to highs and lows. But we must always look for the dream of our youth, the fulfillment of the calling, even though we know in advance it's going to be a roller-coaster ride. Nothing hurts like rejection. And the truth is this. In the worst year of their young lives, the love and the surprise acknowledgement from a random group of people felt like the biggest group hug I've ever witnessed. Again, it felt like sheer support. And in times of loss, the only thing we can do for others is to pray and show support. This momma is and was thankful for every person who has loved on my girls.

The road life was busy, Stronger On Tour was thriving. It was the perfect platform for me in this new season. I could exhort, sing, a little or a lot. The bench was deep; there's a lot of us. The girls were being used in a mighty way as well. The family support was helpful. There's no time for a setback when you're busy and surrounded by a dozen people on a 45-foot bus!! The triggers that sent me reeling were becoming fewer and fewer, and we were seeing a Christian counselor. All three of the girls were benefitting, and I certainly was too. It's an expensive decision, but for us it was and is necessary. I can't endorse this decision enough. At first, I procrastinated with the choice to commit to the scheduling and the financial commitment. But in retrospect, it's been a game changer. It takes work to learn to live your life in a broken world. It takes work to learn how to remain hopeful in an environment of grief. It takes work to learn how to forgive the unforgivable and free yourself from the chains of bitterness. It is all HARD work. But I attempted to insulate myself from the ugly cloak of bitterness through the commitment to the hard work of working on me. You see, we can't change anyone, only ourselves. None of us can help what happened to us. But we can certainly decide how to respond to it. The word of God is full of promises. We already know what He will do. But what will we do? That's the big question. If you've been through trauma, if you've been subjected to life-altering pain, I beg you. Find someone to help you. I am so glad we did. October was the month that I realized just how far we had all come!!!

On a beautiful October day, three of my high-school

friends, from Kentucky, came to Tennessee!! I spent the day with them, and maybe for the first time since January 11th, I felt hopeful in a personal way. I'm always hopeful in a Jesus way. But I felt the confidence come back in me, the woman, or the girl, or whatever I am. I felt the sheer joy of friendship, the blessings of laughter, coffee, cupcakes, and fall pumpkins. That was the day that I suddenly noticed how pretty the pumpkin patch was, the orange and golden yellow against the blue sky. I was leaving the zone that's called simply surviving, and I was stepping over into the zone of thriving. It felt good, and it had been a long time coming!! My random moments of anxiety were starting to be replaced with random moments of joy!!

And the month of October is special to me because my baby girl was born on the 17th. Gracelynn Kelly entered the world with a bang, that's for sure. It's a long miracle story, and maybe one for another time, but the bottom line is this. Her life is nothing short of a miracle. I had just started the labor process on the morning of October 17th. They had admitted me and started the Pitocin drip. Without explanation a nurse came in and said, " I just feel like I need to check you!!" She may or may not have known, but that was the Holy Ghost!! The umbilical cord had prolapsed. That nurse called for help, stayed on my bed, physically holding the cord so that the oxygen wasn't completely deprived. I now know that many babies that have cord prolapse don't survive or they end up with a life-altering condition. On that day this rock star of a nurse stayed in that position, never moving her hand, until they did an emergency C-section and got Gracie out. She literally saved her life. I believe the enemy was scared of this one and that God ordered the steps of that nurse!!

Gracie is as perceptive as a 30-year-old, with the personality of a talk show host. I'm aware of a seasoning, a bit of a retreat in her personality, but I'm convinced that it's a season. I think the sassy version may show back up!! Ha!!

So on the night before her birthday, we gathered in our little blue house. The celebrations of the year had been a little more low-key than in years past. She wanted chicken potpie, so Blaine offered to prepare her favorite meal. We ate, celebrated our Gracie, and I truly thanked God for the people that God had placed around me to show her love.

I was beginning to realize that I had to walk into the future with the ability to celebrate a holiday, or a birthday, with or without the flood of memories, and actually be okay. The triggers that brought about anger had to be kept in check. When you're the one that's rejected, and a divorce happens, it's so easy to despise all things that he/she was a part of.

But you know it's getting better, when there's a few inside jokes, a few moments of laughing through it, instead of crying through it. I love to laugh, and I love to make people laugh!! I've been known to watch a funny video and gut-laugh for an hour. It's in my DNA. We think so many things and so many people are funny, around our house. And it was truly getting better; we were moving toward the mark of acceptance. Gracie's birthday was truly pretty much okay, trigger free for me.

The month finished off with a very busy road schedule and rush to finish the new Christmas album that the girls were doing. We also booked a 12-city tour to coincide with the release of that Christmas album. Times were fast-paced, but again. It was just what the doctor ordered. 2021 will go down in history as being the worst of times, and the best of times.

Peace I leave with you; my peace I give you. I do not give to you as the world gives. Do not let your hearts be troubled and do not be afraid.

A Different November

As November rolled around, our first week ended with the awful news that my sweet Aunt Anneta had passed away. She was much more than an aunt to us. She had almost been in the role of a grandmother for my entire life. She was Mom's older sister, by 14 years, Mom's number one influence, and the reason I like carrot cake and black-and-white polka-dot anything. She exuded class and taste. Her life had been riddled with sickness, accidents, and lots of heart surgeries from a defective heart valve. But she ALWAYS pulled through. We called her a cat, because she had been at death's door so many times. Actually, it seemed that she had more than nine lives. It was more like 20 or

– 124 –

30. So when Mom said that she was declining, we all thought: This is Anneta. She will surprise us all. But she didn't. On the morning of November 8th she changed addresses. At 79 years old, the lady that had inherited the job as matriarch of Mom's family went to her eternal home, and I know that my sweet little grandmother was waiting for her with a hug and that smile!!! On the morning of November 12th, our family gathered in Beaver Dam, Kentucky, to honor her.

The night before her funeral we had a Stronger tour date in Kentucky. Sometimes I think God is generous concerning the details of travel. We decided we wouldn't cancel the Stronger service, as we knew that Anneta wouldn't have wanted it any other way!! We're always committed to the promise of going, walking out the path that's planned months in advance for our ministry purpose. So the fact that it was in Kentucky was really helpful for the routing!! God had to have been in that detail.

So the night before we went to Corbin, Kentucky, and praised and worshipped, then turned those two buses west and headed to Beaver Dam. I was tired, sad, and had dreaded this day so very much!! But we wanted to honor her with her wishes. If anyone deserved honor, she did!!! I had been asked to speak, and I was SO honored, but I was nervous. I HAD to get it right. She had loved me so unconditionally, she was such a big part of me, so I pressured myself more than ever. As I spoke on that beautiful fall day, standing at the end of her casket looking at my family, the words of this verse became an overwhelming TRUTH, as we assessed her 79 years of living:

I Corinthians 14: 4-5 Love is patient, love is kind, it does not envy, it does not boast, it is not proud. It does not dishonor others, it is not self-seeking, it is not easily angered, it keeps no record of wrongs.

It struck me that the loss was deeper than I would realize for many years. I knew I would miss her more with time. The tears flowed freely; we had all suffered tremendous loss.

As Thanksgiving was approaching, I told Mom, "I want to gather at my new house on Thanksgiving Day. We need to make happy memories here. We need this house to be associated with celebration." It had been a safe haven, but I wanted to dig deep and find a way to celebrate in it. As I said, the year of grief had been pushed back with busy schedules and very little time to think. But it was coming. The moment of truth would come when the holidays came. The closer we got, the more the dread set in. I knew that the gatherings, the Christmas and Thanksgiving season in general, would inevitably shine a light on the loss the girls and I were experiencing. We were in the place that I call "imperfect progress." Three steps forward, two backward, four forward, one backward, etc. Grief is so tricky. Grief without closure is even trickier. And I'm told that the grief that comes when someone chooses this can be worse than death on those who are left behind. When we assess the change, it's severe. My home, my work, my parenting, my ministry, every single aspect of my life has been touched. As the thoughts of settling in and being at home for a week, I knew I had to manage this time correctly. We all know that holidays are the most depressing days of the year for those with built-in sadness. It's very tough to fake it in front of your kids. We may fake it at work, or at church, but when we get home, they know. I had to establish what the formula was for us to get through the next six weeks or so and finish the year with some good that was worthy of competing with the bad.

My mom came over the night before Thanksgiving and prepared all of the food for the next day. She put the turkey on, made desserts, all of the things that you do. If you know me, you know I will admit I am not an amazing cook; I want to be, I plan to be, but I am not there yet!! My mom, however, can throw it down; as we say in the South. She is known for her southern cooking, and I always say that her green beans are the absolute best!!!

A few days before Thanksgiving, I was determined to get a Christmas tree! We had always gone really big at Christmas at our house. That was mostly Mike's thing. Way over-the-top decorations for starters, like four or more trees, lights everywhere inside and out, and a Santa Claus on every shelf, like dozens upon dozens!! It was over-the-top. I am still struggling with having a Santa. I may never own one again. The girls were struggling with those childhood memories, and I knew I had to make very different choices. I wanted something that would not remind us of the past. I made up my mind I would get a very classy, simple tree. The first two attempts to buy one ended with me in tears, standing clueless, in an aisle for 30 minutes just staring at the options, wondering how I wound up HERE, ALONE...PICK-ING out a tree. It was as if every single Christmas memory that was stored in temporal lobe exploded into my thought process and flooded my mind. The memories of bringing home our firstborn on Christ-mas Eve, to hearing the laughter of my girls around the tree opening American Girl dolls, the memories kept rolling like a loop of Mike, all the Santas, and visuals of Christmases past. I couldn't do this!!! Here came the tears!! No tree today.

I left frustrated with myself, not once, but twice;

why wasn't I stronger? Just when I thought I was GOOD, here come those darn triggers!! Understanding the process helped a little. Grief DOES come in waves. It's unpredictable to a point, but ALWAYS has triggers. Clearly Christmas, trees, and Santas are triggers for us.

I was approaching a year, and yet I was still crumbling when something reminded me. OH NO!! I had to do better. I gave myself grace, of course, but I always ended up with that same question: "How DID I get here? How did I miss it? Why wasn't it what I thought it was?" I may never know those answers, and I am learning to accept that. God doesn't always give us all of that information, and people rarely do. So, we surrender daily, we surrender the need for all of the answers, we surrender the urge to self-sabotage ourselves for not knowing what we didn't know, for trusting blindly in people that led us straight into heartbreak. And we try to BUY a tree!!

My cousin Jessica came to visit from Ohio that same week. She has a family knack for all things related to décor. She is Anneta's granddaughter, so it's the DNA. Mom has it, Hope has it, as well as Krystal. Great taste, just naturally. We were at Home Goods while she was here, and I was sharing a little about my struggle. Before I knew it, we had picked out a beautiful, simple tree, and the most beautiful simple ornaments. It was perfect, exactly what I needed, feminine and the opposite of years prior. It may seem small, and unimportant, but God knew I needed sweet little Jesse, He knew my heart's desire was to never have my girls look back and think that I refused to celebrate our life, or the Christmas season, because MY LIFE WAS difficult!! We loved that tree when it was in the corner of the living room of that little blue house. How thankful I am for the people that God gave me. When life is this tough it's always easy to know who your people are. They're the ones that are willing to help. It may seem like a small thing to help someone choose a tree, but it matters. When we give of our time and support, we are giving the greatest gift we have.

We cleaned the house, Mom cooked enough for an army, and my house was the gathering place for the family on Thanksgiving!! It wasn't sad. It was actually great. We ate, gathered around the piano and sang, laughed a lot, and as with all Thanksgivings, I went to bed a bit exhausted, a little too full, and with a very grateful heart. We had made it a year past the horrible start of this nightmare, the phone call that was the first piece of this awful puzzle. I was amazed that we were all healthy, able to laugh, and in our right minds. But even more amazed that we had been miraculously sustained financially. I have always known that gratitude makes anything enough. But I knew on this day that I was beyond blessed.

I want to insert this thought as I wrap up this chapter. I feel that praise is a key to getting through. We had spent a year of public humiliation, sometimes just showing up...only to find out that God had shown up way before us and prepared a people that would remind us that we were loved, and that uninhibited love gave us the bravery to shed our shame, our humiliation, and put the full armor of God on, and find the praise that we came to bring. You see, the Lord knows when you're too broken to go, but you go anyway. He knows you've lost sleep, sold your ring to pay the electric bill, borrowed money from your family to buy your child's medicine. He also knows that you know how to find a private moment to sing so loud it's scary, to praise until the tears come, He knows you. He knows you're in it to win it. You may not be broke, maybe you're sick, maybe you're in a mess and don't know how to get out. Maybe YOU did it, maybe YOU created the hell of the moment. Whatever your moment of humanity looks like. We all have the ability to tap into the **formula of praise. And praise is the key. A thankful heart wants to praise. Can we praise our way out of hell? Yes, you can.**

I will forevermore tell people that the key to getting through most things is to rear back and praise Him. Don't be shy. Let it rip!! Tell Him that circumstances look bad, but you're fully aware that He's good. And that daily you're looking to be loaded down with the benefits that belong to you!

We made it through, and our hearts were so full of thanks in November!! He had kept us.

I will give thanks to you, Lord,
with all my heart;
I will tell of all your wonderful deeds.
I will be glad and rejoice in you;
I will sing the praises of your name,
O Most High.

Psalm 9:1–2

It's December Again

The girls and I were about to go on a Christmas tour, band in tow, my mom and Steve with us. My mom, always thinking ahead, realized we needed to keep ourselves EXTRA busy during this season. Sometimes an idle mind is the devil's playground. Actually an idle mind is always the devil's playground!! I had heard this saying my whole life, but I never truly understood until this year. The girls recorded a Christmas EP produced by Blaine and Ben Isaacs. This tour had them doing most of the singing, and I joined them throughout the set for a few songs. It was fun! They crushed it. Their musical growth was happening right before my eyes. This evolution was birthed out of necessity, but it was a gift to be there to see it. The tour highlighted their vocal capabilities. Christmas songs are the most complicated songs to sing. The intricate parts that they had arranged for the album were vocally complex. I was amazed and, as a singer, totally impressed at the ease that they had during the first rehearsal. It was truly their element. The intricate inversions, the swelling and moving harmony parts, it was musical joy!! I watched them sing night after night, and I was constantly reminded that the tough times are so much easier when we have made the decision that nothing or no one can steal our song!!

God uses ALL seasons to build us into who we are meant to be for HIS purpose. So the Christmas season of 2021 was one of musical molding and stretching, tour exhaustion, and lots of bus fun!! We laughed on that crowded bus every single night! I saw my sweet girls experience so MUCH joy on that tour. It was wonderful to see that again. We took a full band out, and the bus was crowded. Typically, that's never a good thing. A dozen dates, back to back, the extra guys in the band, Cameron my niece was there too, plus Mom and Steve, and of course my crew and the girls. The band was the Stronger band, so we were well acquainted, but they had never toured on my bus. They typically rode the other bus that's Mom and Steve's. Mom and Steve sold a property and bought a bus in early 2021 in order to be able to help facilitate Stronger and the transportation needs. So these guys were typically over there. I hadn't thought about it a lot, prior to this Christmas run. In reality, there wasn't much time to think at all in that busy season. These guys are adult men with jobs, lives, and do not fit the profile of a touring musician, I suppose. They're there because they want to be. Their musicianship is excellent, the best of the best. But they were all seasoned professionals who had morphed into successful careers, otherwise. I felt incredibly blessed to have them, and I think I reminded the girls to give them space and make sure they kept their things in their own space. You know what girls are like. Cosmetic bags everywhere, hair dryers, curling irons, flat irons, 100 pairs of shoes, clothes, jewelry, and you name it—they had it, the apple don't fall far from the tree!! Ha! We had shopped for festive clothes; they desperately needed them. I did everything in my power to keep them looking forward, and occasionally that meant clothes, hair, nails, or new makeup. A sweet friend sent them money for clothes for the tour, and we shopped!!

So, on night one, we packed the bus like sardines and headed down the road. The mood was especially good. The girls were nervous about their vocals, but made it through like champs. They didn't miss a move. Oh my, what a beautiful sight it was to see them in their element. Each anticipating the vocal movement of the other, almost like they had rehearsed for months. Yet, I knew they had rehearsed very little. There wasn't time. I watched and realized the depth of their talent. I pray I don't sound like a bragging mom right now. Ha! But this was another vocal level for them, and they did it flawlessly. No wonder the enemy wanted to break them. They have a future. The second night was better, the third night even better, and by the fourth night, it was as if they had been singing these songs for 10 years. On about the fifth day, I realized what a great time they were having. I hadn't heard them laugh like that in a year. I hadn't seen them interact with people, who weren't family, with that much ease in such a long time. The walls were coming down. They were learning to have fun anyway. Katelanne was giggling, Gracie was begging Poppa Steve to let her fix his hair, and Hope was listening intently as they sat in the front lounge and told funny church stories!! We all know that God places people in the balcony of our life to cheer when we need a little extra. These people had watched us, me and the girls, for eight long months, on the Stronger tour. They saw us wipe mascara, have meltdowns, and at times they wiped tears when I would tell my story. I suppose it's safe to say they that were invested in our well-being. They were cheering from the balcony, always! As this tour rolled down the highway,

I was reminded of how God orders our steps. He places us where we need to be, at the oddest times. These guys, who got up early and worked their jobs from hotel lobbies, using Zoom and their computers, were certainly planted in our lives for that season. They were tired, I'm sure, but they stayed the course. And in my heart, I believe they filled up the emptiness that sometimes loomed. It's funny how God sends people to us, sometimes only for a season, and sometimes for a lifetime of friendship. What a special season this one was. My heart is full as I remember.

I truly want to thank every single person who has been a part of this healing process. You know who you are.

We finished up the tour and went home to our little blue house. The high of the tour was over, and there seemed to be a bit of sadness from the girls, now on to the reality of life. When you're in the craziness of the road, reality is foreign sometimes. The travel and business takes precedence over so many things. The tour had served us well. We had nearly gotten through the month!

Back in October, on a lark and a real estate conversation with Mom, Steve, and Cameron, Hope decided to buy a house. Steve knew that the market was changing fast, and he knew that they would be unable to buy if they didn't do it quick. Steve has been a Nashville real estate broker for 30-plus years. This story is actually amusing. Cameron is Hope's age, her cousin, built-in friend, and is full of common sense. She knew it was time to buy. She and Hope were both buying houses at this point. Cameron had decided a few days before Hope that she had to get in the market or be left behind. The prices here in Nashville are horrendous and getting worse by the minute. Everyone wants to live here, much to my dismay. The traffic is awful, and I for one won't attempt to go downtown on most days. It's a traffic nightmare!! But it's home. And Hope felt that she could handle the challenge. And my thoughts are this. I'd rather see her paying for a home than buying useless items. I knew she was responsible enough to do this on her own. Again, we have been blessed with lifetime relationships. Our family has been blessed with people who caught the vision that comes with crazy ministry dreams. One of these people is a banker. He's a lifetime friend. One call and a common sense conversation, and he was on board with these girls, and they were approved to be homeowners. But the funniest part? About a month later, they decided to switch houses!! Not kidding. Appraisals were done and the paperwork was flowing. But the houses weren't quite finished yet. Just like they used to switch dresses, when they were three years old, they now wanted to switch houses. Ha!!! How do you do that?? Steve said it couldn't be done. But after a couple of hours on the phone, a lot of explaining, they brought everyone into agreement. The representative for one of the builders said, "Your family seems a little crazy, but I'm here for it!!" Ha!! Perfectly said.

So, four days before Christmas, Hope turned 22. She also closed on her first house!! And yes, the switch happened. She moved out the week of Christmas. It was bittersweet. And as I look back, I can't believe I didn't have a complete meltdown. But I didn't. I knew how good this was for her. I knew how proud she was. And the truth is, it was a great distraction. The year of hell had pushed her up a couple of notches in maturity. So her happiness was my happiness. Several members of my family called and said, "Are you okay?" Everyone expected me to fall apart when she left. But it didn't happen. Maybe it's because she's five minutes away. Ha!!

She's such a good girl, and she has been a voice of reason in the worst season of our lives. How I've appreciated her stability. At her age she could be doing anything! But this girl believes in morality and has been everything I ever wanted a daughter to be. Her gifts are amazing, but more than that, she's kind. So, in the midst of the year of change, we celebrated Hope's birthday and her first little home!! We thanked the Lord for the provision provided for her to buy that little house. It was truly another miracle that won't be fully appreciated until she's older!!

When she could have retreated to the depression that wanted to own her, she could have chosen isolation, addiction, or any other vice in the devil's plethora of choices, she didn't. Instead, she decided to step up, grow up, and be a stabilizing force in all of our lives. I'm thankful.

It was our first Christmas with just me and the girls, our family of five was now four, but we made it. I put together a schedule that was intentional in every way. We had a different kind of Christmas. But we were together. And that was enough for this momma. We made it.

I won't pretend it was a Hallmark movie; it was hard, it was sad, it was unusual, but it doesn't mean God is not STILL good or that His promises have changed. You learn that every step in the process matters. Picking out your first tree, shopping alone, decorating alone. It all matters, you owe it to yourself to not only survive, but to thrive. Sometimes we must fight for it. Cry through it. But we are worth it. We do it for us, not the one that left. We pick the tree, even if we don't want one. We make the meal, even if we're not hungry. Sometimes we're just proving to ourselves that we CAN GET through it!! The truth is, not everyone can go where you're going. Sometimes people choose a path that separates.

There's never been a tear, a sleepless night, or a day of loneliness...that's wasted.

Overall, December was good to us.

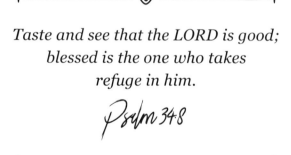

Taste and see that the LORD is good;
blessed is the one who takes
refuge in him.

Psalm 34:8

Oh January,
Here You Are Again

We ended December with a great big surprise!! Mom rented a cabin for the entire family in Gatlinburg, that was part of our intentional planning. We had Christmas on Christmas Day at her house, and then we were all to meet at the cabin on the 26th. I was plagued with a few symptoms, but didn't think much of it. Allergies had been raging. We walked in the house at Christmas, and Jason immediately said he didn't feel well either. Again, not much thought of it. We were all exhausted. December had been incredibly busy, for the entire family. If I listed all of the things that we did, you wouldn't believe it. In addition to the tour, we had hosted a Stronger retreat in the mountains. We had been with thousands of people in December.

But on Christmas night we ate turkey and dressing with giblet gravy, cranberry sauce, glazed ham, and all of the trimmings, and I was thankful for family. We went home and loaded the car.

On the morning of the 26th, we left, headed to Gatlinburg, and looking forward to it. This seemed like a great idea. A cabin for 35, a view, hot chocolate, and board games. What could be better? We all arrived and settled in. I felt worse. Katelanne wasn't feeling well. Long story short, our Christmas present? Covid. Round two for most of us! I tested the morning after I arrived and I was positive. I went home immediately. Most of the family had it and didn't know it.

We quarantined, cancelled a few dates, and stayed at home. It was cold!! We had a bit of snow, and I settled into the job of feeling better. Covid was milder this time, and I did fine. Everyone did. I was thankful. There had been so much death in our circle. When I think about the awful devastation and loss of life that came with Covid, it wrecks me. What a terrible time in history this has been.

And in my life, the anniversary of the confession was coming. Emotionally, I braced for it. It was crazy when I allowed myself to think about it. I hadn't seen him in a year. When I thought about it, I realized that seeing him would be like seeing a ghost. It was so hard to believe. However, January 11th came, and there was very little notice. I was busy, and as I've said repeatedly, that helps.

I MADE IT!! I had survived. I had waited for this day. I had prayed for this day.

And now, it was here: the one-year anniversary of weathering this awful storm that came to take us down. Should we make a cake? Should we get up and dance? Should I allow myself to have a good cry? What does one do on a day like this?

What did we do? We lived. We walked out our new normal, knowing we would never go back to what was, but could thrive in what was to come.

That which was sent to kill me didn't kill me at all. It made me dig deep and find the faith that I so readily spoke of. That faith that I've sung about since I was a child. I had to find a greater portion of it. Then, I had to make up my mind. I had the tools, the support, and the Lord was clearly making a way.

But somehow, the rejection was the hardest thing for me. I had to learn to put on the full armor, lace up my boots, and purposely imagine myself winning this war. Sometimes we struggle with understanding the Father's love when people have betrayed us. The truth is always the truth. He won't leave. He's faithful. And His goodness is running after us when we are so terrified that all we know to do is run.

The summary of this entire book is simple: GOD WASTES NOTHING.

You think your story is too messy, and you can never use it to glorify Jesus? I would challenge you on that. We must tell our stories. We give our story of hope to the next broken-down life.

Sometimes, it's the story of celebrating a small victory, like finding a Christmas tree. Other times, it's the miracle of the provision that only He could bring. The big things and the small things, it all matters. When HE brings you through, tell it. Testify.

I weighed the impact of telling my story. Some said I should, some will say I shouldn't.

I couldn't get away from it. I had to do it. God said, "We overcome by the word of our testimony."

So here it is. I've done my best. As you have read

about my recent journey, I pray that you are of the opinion that if I can get through it? So can you. He WILL walk that road that you are traveling, alongside you, no matter what it is.

He will keep you. That's the unbelievable thing. This story is about me, but it's also about a million other women who have been rejected, forgotten, and thrown away.

As for me and my girls: I believe that the best is yet to come. I truly believe that.

I don't have it all figured out, and I don't ALWAYS have it all together. I still have so many questions!! I'm not sure what my next five months looks like, much less five years from now. Nevertheless, THIS IS MY STORY, and I believe that telling it will heal me, and I pray it will help you to heal as well.

The tongue has the power of life and death, and those who love it will eat its fruit.

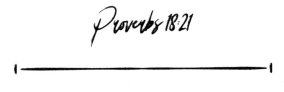

The Hallway

The truth is divorce changes everything. Everything looks and feels different, and nothing looks the way you had hoped it would. For the one that wanted to be married, divorce is complete disappointment. And there's this. There is a chance of being triggered at almost any function you attend. Obviously at weddings, but also at graduations, parties, or just sitting in church without the person that you are used to being beside, can be shockingly hard at times.

This week, as we are at the beach as a family of four, I am reminded of how everything has changed. For a moment I almost allowed sadness to visit, but then I had a moment. We pentecostals might call it a Holy Ghost moment, or Holy Spirit moment if you're more dignified than I am. Ha!!

Anyway, it was like the Spirit said to me, "Why do you keep viewing it as broken?"

I thought to myself, "Because it is!!!"

I am a divorced woman. My children live in what some would refer to as a broken home. But is it broken? I contend that it's beautifully broken in order to allow the miracle of restoration to be on display. Did God intend for my life to be this way? No. But as with all sad stories, we must deal with the human condition and the choices of people. In those stories too, God will be glorified. God is bigger than my brokenness, He's bigger than my hurt, and there will be so much to celebrate in the room at the end of this hallway.

Just because your life hasn't gone in the direction you had hoped for doesn't mean it's going in the wrong direction. There are a thousand ways to get to Tennessee. Sometimes the route changes, depending on the unforeseen detours. But I'm here to tell you, a girl in a pair of cowboy boots, with a guitar strapped to her back, is going to get to Nashville. Her mind is made up. She'll take the backroads and cross the creek if necessary, either way she's getting to town; Music City awaits her. I want to be like that determined girl. I want to find the road to my tomorrow, and this book is part of my journey. It was necessary.

God can clear a path, flip the script, or make a detour anywhere, anytime He sees fit. I'm here for it, patiently waiting while I'm in this hallway.

It's impossible to walk from the grief stricken room that we've been living in, to the room that God has prepared for us, without the hallway transition. The dreaded walk of patience is often learned in the time spent there. We need to forgive and it's usually there that we find forgiveness. In order to grow properly, we must learn to honor the space between the past and the future.

That long hallway feels like a safe place at times, and like a dreaded claustrophobic place at other times. But the truth is always the truth. The hallway season allows us to walk slowly without falling down unexpected steps. It's a time to heal and look back at the room you left and reflect on how far He's brought you. In this hallway, I am realizing that my broken life will be beautiful.

As I finish and finalize my thoughts I want to

publicly acknowledge the consequences of my choices. I've been told over and over that no one walks this kind of thing out publicly. I've been criticized for not taking time off, and I've been shamed for facing this publicity monster head on. I didn't hire a publicist, nor did I hide from the awful intrusive questions. I have attempted to answer with a polite "just pray" without giving details. Why? Why would a person who has never faced much controversy choose this path? I knew I had to pick my "awful". There were no easy answers, there were no comfortable solutions, just the choice of which "awful" I would endure.

I could have chosen the awful path of parking the bus, removing the platform that is in place for my children, and allowing my calling to be negated and my voice to be silent. I could have chosen that "awful."

But as I've said, there's a pentecostal version of me that is pretty much in charge. She rose up on that cold January day when decisions were being made.

As the family came and went, I took counsel and listened to encouragement. I knew that the battle of living this kind of traumatic story in real time, in living color, in front of the public, would ultimately be the challenge of a lifetime.

But I chose that "awful" instead of the life of regret that would surely come if I had chosen the "awful" of quitting. If you have prayed and encouraged me in this journey, thank you. If you've sent me a message and said, "I too am living in the hellish season, and you've strengthened me with your candor," thank you for taking the time to tell me. Your responses have been nothing short of medicine at times. Being candid ain't for sissies, and yes, this has been hard.

Nevertheless, I don't regret the choice.

And finally, let me address those who often ask me about Mike. He's the father of my beautiful children, and I wish him no harm. I have forgiven him, and I pray that he finds his peace.

Surely your goodness and love will follow me all the days of my life, and I will dwell in the house of the LORD forever.